EMBRACING THE EMERGING PROPHETS

Published by:
Keith B. Ferrante
6391 Leisure Town Rd.
Vacaville, CA 95687

Ferrante, Keith B. (2017-04-16).
Embracing the Emerging Prophets
ISBN-13: **978-1545451618**
ISBN-10: **1545451613**
Cover Designer: Shelby Gibbs

Endorsements

Keith's book is anointed. When I first started reading it I couldn't stop, it had the honey of heaven on it. This is a write that will become prophetic curriculum soon. I felt like it was a prophetic mirror that Keith had placed before the eyes of the reader to get an outward and inward view of their soul and spirit. Not only can you get a clear view of yourself but also those around you that are shaping the Kingdom. This book brought me to the edge of tears because of the content and how well it reflected Keith's heart. What a thrill to see, hear and read the wisdom of God that Keith is stewarding so well. As I read this book it reminded me of reading Bill Johnsons book "When Heaven Invades Earth" before it was published and before he was well known all over the planet and his book became a household book for encounter. This book has the same power!

Wendell McGowan
www.wendellmcgowan.org

For many years, Keith has not only encouraged me as a friend but as a true prophet in our generation. He is a catalytic new breed prophet that is reforming the current prophetic culture as we know it. God has raised him up to equip and mature the prophetic movement with a fresh new perspective from the heart of God. "Embracing the Prophets" releases fresh insight and foresight of what God is doing with prophets today. This book will challenge leaders on how to nurture and steward emerging prophets while maturing those who are walking in the prophetic. This book trumpets the sound of a new prophetic reformation! Get ready for a prophetic upgrade! I highly recommend this book!

Tony Kim
Senior Leader of Renaissance International
Roar Network

In his insightful book, Embracing the Emerging Prophets, Keith Ferrante addresses the mind- sets and value systems that hinder prophetic voices from being heard, and lays down a helpful path to growth and effectiveness.

Keith reveals personal experiences to illustrate that the journey to significance as leaders and prophets must begin with an accurate perspective of our value in the eyes of the Father and lived out in the context of community.

Embracing the Emerging Prophets is a helpful guidebook for prophets, emerging prophets, and those who are privileged to minister with them.

Deborah Crone
Care of David Crone
www.davecrone.com
www.imissionchurch.com

Foreword

Having been elected pastors in their early twenties, Keith and Heather had already been leading a local church for many years when I met them. They pastored a healthy little church in Willits at the gateway to the giant redwood trees. The couple impressed me immediately as powerful worshippers, passionate leaders, and cultural influencers. The only problem was - they were not pastors. I'm not saying that they were not doing a good job at loving and leading people because they truly were, but it was obvious that their gift or office callings were not as pastors of a local church.

As our relationship grew, I remember a strategic conversation Keith, Heather, and I had at a little Italian restaurant. By this time, I believe it had become apparent to the two of them that pastor was not their primary office call. I asked them the question, "If time and money were not an issue, what would the two of you be doing?" The couple quickly responded that they would base them-selves out of a local church from which they could travel, run schools, and train leaders. A few months later they were doing that very thing from our local church, The Mission.

One of the powerful aspects about living in prophetic community is that sometimes the people around you are better at defining who you are and what you are good at than you are yourself. As Keith and Heather faithfully served in various areas of the local church a sweet spot revealed itself. Keith possessed all the raw gifts and graces of an office prophet. Though the couple was incredibly talented at anything they put their hands to, their greatest fruit and sustainability came when their assignments were in line with their prophetic gifting's.

I watched Keith and Heather deliver timely and strategic prophetic words and counsel to a Hollywood movie star, a struggling pastor, an influential doctor, a military general and a millionaire businessman, to name a few. Whenever I met people and mentioned the couple, they would talk about a significant prophetic word they had received. It was then that I asked Keith to lay aside other gifts and talents and focus on staying in the center stream of his prophetic call.

Keith took on the task of creating an advanced prophetic track for high-level prophetic gifts and emerging prophets. He developed prophetic resources for training prophets in their gifts and calling but also a discipleship program that dealt with personal character issues, relational skills, and past wounds. Keith and Heather committed themselves to creating a healthy company of emerging prophets. Though we still have a long way to go on this journey, we are seeing and celebrating some amazing first fruits of contending for a prophetic community.

Ephesians 2:20 says that the church is "Built upon the foundation of apostles and prophets." At some point, we in the church must decide if that statement is a historical narrative or a current man-date. After all, the office of prophet is not only mentioned in an Old Testament context but is vitally included in the list of ascension gifts—those directly related to the time following the ascension of Jesus. (See Ephesians 4:8,11.) I truly believe it is time now for prophets and apostles to arise and help us all form a firm foundation for the reformation of the church.

As Keith mentions in this book, for years we have been comfortable calling every local church leader "pastor," but can we grow comfortable calling out prophets? How do we find them? How will we train them? What will they do? Without prophets, the church will not have a proper foundation. Without prophets, believers are less likely to know the heavenly identity of their new creation. Without prophets, how will the church be encouraged, edified, and comforted? God set prophets in his church, but our religious forms in ignorance and through neglect have largely removed them. It is time for a revival of the church Jesus Christ built. It is time to recognize that, truly, there are prophets amongst us.

In this book, Keith awakens our hearts to the call of finding and raising up prophets among us. With great vulnerability, he shares his own failures and frustrations in discovering his personal call as an emerging prophet. I have walked with Keith in his own emerging prophet role. He has walked closely with me in mine. Now, we are walking together with a great company of emerging prophets to release the grace of hearing, seeing, feeling, and perceiving all that the Spirit of the Lord is saying to His church. My prayer is that this book will reveal the call and the courage within you to find emerging prophets.

Dan McCollam
The Mission, Vacaville, California,
Bethel School of the Prophets,
Author of *Prophetic Company*, *The Good Fight*, and *Basic Training in Prophetic Activation.*

Acknowledgements

I want to give a huge thank you to Angie Parsons for your many hours of editing. You are such a blessing to me. I also want to thank Tom Parsons for formatting this book, and the many things it takes to get this book ready, uploaded and going to print. You guys both are absolutely a huge blessing. I pray rich blessings on you both for your many sacrifices!!

I want to thank a few of the prophets that have believed in me and coached me for many years. Wendell McGowan, Kris Vallotton, Dan McCollam, Martin Scott, to name just a few. Also apostle David Crone, your many hours of speaking into me and creating room for me to grow. Without each of you guys I wouldn't be where I'm at today. Thanks for believing in me. To my lovely wife Heather Ferrante thank you for standing alongside of me as I've grown into my calling. I know it isn't easy to live with a strong prophetic personality such as myself. Without your encouragement, love, and wisdom I wouldn't be where I'm at today. I love being on the journey of life with you, and our lovely children, Maci and Micah!

Finally, Jesus thanks for being the lover of my soul, and the ultimate coach. You have helped me learn how to be a disciple, a lover, a son, and a friend of God. I'm forever yours.

Table of Contents

Introduction

This book is specifically for but not limited to leaders of local churches and those looking to explore if they are called to be a prophet. My hope in writing this book is that you will get excited with me to encourage the many developing prophets that are all around you and even some of you reading this book that are one of those emerging leaders. There is a new epic season that God is opening up to us, and we have to be ready for it. The last twenty to thirty years we have seen the reemergence of the prophetic, the supernatural, and the goodness of God. I'm so excited about that. Now the level of the prophetic in the body of Christ worldwide is at a much higher level. There are hundreds of supernatural schools all over the world, training people in the gift of prophecy and how to walk in the supernatural. Thousands of churches have embraced the prophetic and God's voice in their meetings, that come through the prophetic gift or prophetic voices. This is so exciting! But it also changes the game. The level of the prophetic has risen, and many people are awakening to the fact that they may have more to offer in their life than just a prophetic gift. They are strongly prophetic, see many things in the Spirit, and there doesn't seem to be many places for them to go outside of being trained in the prophetic gift and going through supernatural schools. I believe this is why the season is changing. The bar has risen.

I get to speak and be a part of some great churches that have hosted moves of God and what I see are hundreds of bored saints now ready for the next level. The next level for some is beginning to discover if they are a prophet or maybe they have a higher-level prophetic gift that needs to be developed. Growing up, I had this belief that prophets were untrainable, that there was no such thing as a prophet among us. A rare few might be able to have access to a prophet, but they were on a large platform or had a significant influence. There were certainly no prophets among us. That has changed. We have to begin to realize as church leaders and as people that are hungry for more, that there are prophets among us. They may be unhealthy, immature, a little weird, extreme, hurt, and rejected but they still are needed. God is changing the season, and now there are many sitting in the seats of church facilities, thoroughly bored and wondering is there more for me. Yes, there is more, which I am certain of. Some are called to walk in a high-level prophetic gift realm outside the church buildings in the marketplace. Others are not sure where they fit, but they sense something inside them that needs more than just an outlet in prophetic gift ministry within a ministry team context on a Sunday morning prayer line.

The goal of this book is to help awaken in your heart the necessity of making room for the prophets that are sitting around us, or even ourselves. If you are a church leader or an emerging prophet this book is written with you in mind. It is meant to help church leader's, of who I also am, understand the importance of raising up the emerging prophets within our congregations. If you are an emerging prophet this book is meant to help you get a grid for what a healthy emerging prophet looks like, so you can accelerate your development and begin to get a target for what you should be growing towards. We can't waste what God is pouring out. He raised the bar of the prophetic in the church, so now it is time to look within the prophetic community and start to call out the prophets among us. I welcome you to go on the journey of discovery with me to find the prophets around us and for some, the prophet within us.

Many blessings to you on this wonderful journey.

Keith Ferrante

Chapter 1
But I'm Not a Famous Prophet

I've spent many years not being a famous prophet. You may wonder why I say that. Here's why. Often, I get sent somewhere to speak in some church where a well-known speaker has canceled. I get a last-minute phone call. Other times I get sent on behalf of one of my spiritual fathers who are better known than I but are unable to speak for a variety of reasons. People and leaders sometimes put me through a quiz of questions asking me who I am, where they can find out more info on me, and why the famous prophet mentor wasn't able to come. When their questions have been satisfied, then they at times graciously, but sometimes warily, have me. Most of the time, after a meeting or two together, they are pleasantly surprised and often have me back numerous times.

For years, this bothered me until I realized that not being famous often times can be a gift from God. This allowed me to come into places and minister without having people stumbling over my notoriety. God seems to like to show up around this kind of heart attitude. It really isn't about how small or big our platform is. What is important is humbly walking out his call in whatever sphere he has assigned to me. Of course, I'm not against notoriety and I'm not even implying that it's prideful. I'm more interested in understanding God's purposes and reasons for where the level of recognition by man is and where it is supposed to be.

Recently for a whole year, I vexed over not being asked to speak at a place I often preach each year. For years, I had been on the regular teaching schedule, but as the leaders made changes in the leadership structure of that church, I and another or two weren't on the circuit anymore to speak. It wasn't that there was something wrong with our teaching; it was just that the leadership was in transition and needed more time in the pulpit. For some reason, this hit a sore spot in me. "Why am I not speaking at this church, Lord?" I asked. I sensed the Lord reply, "I've saved the best wine till last." That wine came at a time I wasn't expecting.

I had devoted two years building a relationship with a leader from another country. He kept telling me he was going to bring me over to speak, but he hadn't yet pulled the trigger. (Later he said it was because he wasn't expecting the presence of God to come out of me like it did when I ministered.) As time went on, he conveyed he wanted to have one of my prophet friends come out instead. Of course, that didn't feel great, but I reluctantly said ok I'll try to make the connection. My prophet friend graciously said he wasn't interested in coming unless I came with him and we ministered together. So, I communicated the information back to the pastor of that nation. Surprisingly the pastor said he'd love to have us both come out. So, he booked our tickets. When we landed in this country, we had dinner with the pastor who gave us the teaching schedule. It showed only my friend preaching. Of course, you know that didn't sit too well with me. I had spent so much time building the relational connection with this leader and had come under the notion that I too would be speaking. Now I found out that I had flown all this way to simply "carry the bags" of my prophet friend. Not a good day for me. I'm not as spiritual as Elisha I guess. Lol. I wanted to go to my room and have a huge pity party. I went to my room and started down the path to do just that, drink down a healthy dose of self-pity.

...What a bitter taste.

Cutting my bitter drink short as if on a queue, (as he always is) a spiritual father prophet from America called me and kindly but quickly told me to get over my pity party. He prophetically spoke that I was in that country to bring much-needed intercession and that my primary job during that short visit was the prayer that happened behind the scenes. He said don't worry about not speaking; your prophet friend will build the wood for the fire every time he speaks, and you will get a chance to speak at the end of the conference to light the fire. Of course, there was no guarantee that would happen, I was not on the speaking schedule, and the pastor that had invited us was only interested in hearing my friend speak.

On his own accord, my friend graciously and firmly told the pastor he wanted me to speak the last session for him. My friend was only interested in opening the door of that nation to me…even if I had to walk the low road for a while to get there. Before the final meeting where I ended up speaking, the Lord said, "I've saved the best wine till last." The Lord's word to me earlier that year had finally arrived. The meetings my friend completed were great, and when I got up to speak, the presence of God rocked the place. It was like my prophet friend said, the wood was built for the fire, and now I got to light the fire. After -ward, the pastor, with bewilderment and wonder in his eyes, was taken back and said; "I didn't know you had that in you, Keith."

Of course, that at times still perplexes me because, humbly, I know what I carry. I recognize that what I have in the Spirit is good. It will touch lives and bring a breakthrough. I've seen it happen over and over. But for some reason, God often has kept me under the radar. If you want to find me on the web, it will take work. There are few online videos out there with my ministry on them, even though I've ministered in many places. I struggled for years with why there seemed to be a lack of notoriety. But God often likes to build his prophets in the desert.

After that trip, I asked the Lord what he was doing in me. "What test am I in Lord?" I inquired. "The test of humility and celebration of other prophet's ministries." He responded. So good, then I knew what was going on. That helped a lot. Once I know what the test is, it is much easier to get in alignment with it. At that point, I was fully aware of what I had to go after. I knew I had to pass this test. It's funny because I train companies of prophets and I tell them all the time that learning where their platform is beyond the Sunday morning pulpit is a great breakthrough for them. But here I was, struggling with the same issue.

Knowing now I needed to pass this test; I expectantly waited for another humility opportunity to come along. Within a day, I had a Facebook message from a long-lost connection asking me how I was doing. They then pointedly asked me if I could help get my prophet friend to their church. The same prophet friend I had just traveled with overseas. Even though I knew this was the test, a small part of me thought but did not verbalize, "I'm not his P.A you know!" But I was resolved to pass this test. I wrote back with all that was in my heart, "Yes, it would be my joy to try to open the door for my friend to speak at your venue." That same day the same thing happened one more time. Another person was trying to go through me to get my friend to speak. I responded the same way. "Yes, I'd love to make the introduction to my prophet friend." It's funny how God does things with us, isn't it? But He is so good and so faithful and rewards us when we understand what He is after. We don't need to be famous or sought after; if we are doing his will, it is enough.

It's great when the reward for the test shows up. The next day the reward for passing the test manifested. I got three unexpected calls. One of those calls was from another country with a last-minute request. Could I come and fill in for a famous prophet who got sick? "Of course, I could," I said, after I briefly prayed and asked the Lord and my wife. Then two more requests came in. God was telling me that I had passed the test. Now He was opening up doors again for me.

An amazing thing was happening to me in this whole process. The desire to be famous was genuinely leaving my motives. I know no good believer tries to keep those thoughts in their mind. No one intentionally thinks I want to be famous, or I want to be somebody. I'd resisted those thoughts for years, but deep down inside they were still there. I guess I was hoping fame would fix the hole in my heart that felt lonely, rejected, and overlooked. God wanted to fix the real issue. He wanted me settled in knowing that I'm enough. In Him I have everything. I needed to get into my spirit I am doing a great job for Him no matter what. Whether I am prophesying over someone behind the scenes, I am prophesying over a city and doing a prophetic act on some gang-ridden streets that no one else will ever see, or whether I am preaching at a church of 15 people and ministering to each of them like they are Kings and Queens of nations. God was doing something in me. He was taking out of me the desire to be famous. It was like during that season of not preaching, I was learning to be thankful for others notoriety and realizing that I am making a difference right where I am.

You see, God is raising up a massive number of prophets and prophetic people who don't need recognition. If we don't realize what He is doing, we are going to miss out on a bunch of great but under the radar prophets who are right in front of us. You'll miss out on him using you or receiving from the amazing person next to you if you're fame-stricken. Paul says in Ephesians 1:18, "I pray also that the eyes of your heart may be enlightened in order that you may know the hope to which he has called you, the riches of his glorious inheritance in the saints." The inheritance is Christ in the saints. Ephesians 4 says, "Christ gave some to be Prophets…" We have to stop looking for the famous prophet who is afar and start recognizing the amazing prophets nearby. There are riches in the hills of the people all around you, and you have incredible riches in you as well. Proverbs 27:10

also says, "… better a neighbor nearby then a brother far away." This next era is about the unknown prophets and the saints walking in astonishing power right amongst us.

You know, it was an unknown prophet that anointed Jehu King who finally ended the reign of Jezebel. 2 Kings 9:1-3 says,

> "The prophet Elisha summoned a man from the company of the prophets and said to him, 'tuck your cloak into your belt, take this flask of oil with you and go to Ramoth Gilead. When you get there, look for Jehu son of Jehoshaphat, the son of Nimshi. Go to him, get him away from his companions and take him into an inner room. Then take the flask and pour the oil on his head and declare, 'This is what the Lord says: I anoint you king over Israel.' Then open the door and run; don't delay!'"

This unknown prophet was simply one of the company of prophets that Elisha picked out, helped him understand what he was supposed to say to the King, and then sent him on his way. The unknown prophet was recognized by Jehu and his cohorts as one of the prophets, but this man was unnamed in scripture. Isn't it more important that we are known by the fruit of what we bring than by the name of the person who delivered the message?

The Jezebels, or the taunting strongholds of our day, are going to be taken down not primarily through well-known prophets, but by yielded prophets who are in a community, connected to other prophets, and teachable. Just as the unknown prophet was able to be given the basic framework on what he was to prophesy to anoint Jehu King, so too will God anoint in this next season - prophets who aren't necessarily famous, but are yielded to Jesus and sent with authority. They will tear down the works of the enemy and will bring glory to Jesus while walking yielded and humble. Let us resolve to be a voice of the Lord, known in heaven, feared in hell, and not worried about notoriety on earth.

In the next chapter, I want to talk about how God uses prophets to impact the world around them through other means besides the pulpit. We are often fixated on the pulpit being what determines success that we are missing the many other kingdom opportunities offered to us regularly.

Chapter 2
Why Don't I Get to Speak At Church?

Sometimes we are so fixated on the church service being the place that everything significant must happen. We think to ourselves, "If only I could speak Sunday or at a special revival meeting, or at my favorite church then I'd finally be somebody."

I grew up in the church, and I'm a third generational pastor. My grandpa pastored, my dad pastored, and I followed suit. It was the thing that was recognized growing up as the ultimate place of being useful in the Kingdom. To preach behind the pulpit, to pastor a church, or to be a missionary was the greatest "call." I grew up in this culture and learned that affirmation came when I filled those shoes. So, I preached, pastored and also did some evangelism and short term missionary work. My wife and I pastored at the young age of twenty-three years old a church of about one hundred folks, the same church my parents pastored. Now don't get me wrong, I love every one of those expressions of ministry. But I know that they are just a few of the many valid and powerful expressions of the Kingdom flowing through the saints.

I saw my unhealthiness when God sent me to another location, Vacaville, to help run a supernatural school and travel to other nations to do ministry. I had a huge identity crisis. I thought, "Who am I outside of being a pastor? Will people respect me if I am not a senior leader?" Many identity challenges hit me.

The problem in our church world is that we are so fixated on pastors and pulpits. The vast majority of people in the Christian world will never see a pulpit. If we don't get unimpressed with the pulpit and pastors, then we are never going to see the reformation and harvest we all want to see. Whatever you affirm, you empower. The lack of affirming ministry that is going on through the saints in daily life, work, family, and the mundane but necessary things has caused the repetitive strongholds that don't get a breakthrough. We wonder why we don't see a breakthrough in our churches and try harder and harder to preach better sermons and have better speakers because we hope that it is the way to bring transformation. In this reformation, God is moving the pulpit from center stage to the back corner. The pulpit will still have a role. But our view of the pulpit will drastically change, and preaching in a church building behind the pulpit will become a smaller part of the transformation needed in the church, not the largest part.

Now don't get me wrong, most of my world is built around the pulpit. I love to preach and spend a lot of time preaching, teaching, and training. But God is up to something different.

Now how does this relate to prophets? We have been way too fixated on teaching prophets. Those are the ones we love to hear. We say, "Wow that is an amazing prophet, he sure taught a very clear and well-articulated message. That was brilliant teaching that prophet gave." If you look through the eighty or so named prophets in the Bible, many of them never preached a single message. Daniel wasn't a preaching prophet. What about Joseph? Esther didn't preach at all. How about Elijah and Elisha? They are demonstration, signs and wonders, and fire prophets, etc. What about King David? He was a prophet King. But most of his prophetic work was done through songs, prayers, and interaction with God one on one. What about Abraham? Was he a prophet? Yes, he was. But, how did he function as a prophet? He functioned as a friend of God. God gave him promises and he then believed God for them to come to pass. That was his role as a prophet - a believing Prophet.

Now there are a lot of great message prophets who have brought, and are needed to continue to bring, teaching to a church, nation, and people group. We so need them, but for some reason, the church has been so fixated primarily on teaching prophets. I'm not sure why we often only recognize prophets when they come in teaching form as a valid expression. That locks those who have another expression as a prophet into trying to fit into something that will never really work for them.

I have a great prophet friend who is an amazing fire prophet. He opens the heavens up through his prophetic gift and can bring breakthrough in a room. But he is not a line-by-line teaching prophet. He is a fire prophet. He talks about this, and that, and to some, it seems random. What is he saying? Now I know him, and I know he is very intentional about what he is going after. But he doesn't fit into the teaching box. So, some write him off. He is not great conference material, some say. He is hard to follow. But he brings a breakthrough of the presence of God in the meeting context.

I think we are wondering where the breakthroughs are in our churches and in the Kingdom expressions around us. I wonder if perhaps it is because we have not allowed the prophets that are not teaching prophets to be released in our midst. Is it because they are so unpredictable? Is it because they make the people we are leading feel uncomfortable? They make us uncomfortable too? That is probably true for a lot of us. We are scared. We have this very "safe" ship we want to keep going the right direction. It is a perfect balance that we must keep or else we could cause some people to leave.

My question is, who is leaving; the presence of God or the presence of people? If you get God and lose a few individuals, was it worth it? If you keep the people but wonder how come you only have a residue of presence, is it worth it? So often, I'm in meetings that are dry. There is anointing when a particular person ministers, preaches or sings. But much of what is going on is not anointed. The sad thing is people are okay with that because they have a few anointed speakers. Is it possible that you can have anointed speakers, worship leaders, etc. and God not be in the place at all? The only thing that keeps the meeting feeling like church at all is that someone that is ministering has a relationship with God, but we are more concerned about having a great relationship with the people and building the numbers in the church.

You see, prophets don't primarily care about great church numbers. They care about a great God being near. The Lord told me years ago, if you are a friend with the King of Kings, you'll have all the Kings of your world as your friend. But if you try so hard to have everybody as your friend, but miss being the King's friend, you've lost it all.

On a similar but different note, God wants to get us from being preoccupied with the church service pulpit and look at where the pulpit really is. What is a pulpit anyways? It's a place of influencing someone. What if the pulpit for influence is wherever you have a voice because you have an authentic message to bring that you are living out? What if the pulpit God is raising up is the pulpit that is in your home, the pulpit at your work or with your neighbors? What if we started seeing that God was moving the pulpit to many other places beyond the church building? Maybe we'd start seeing a move of God.

Prophets throughout the Bible often made a greater impact outside the meeting than within a meeting. Daniel influenced Kings and altered the course of a nation through correctly interpreting dreams. Elisha began to bring Israel back to God because of his prayers and prophetic acts, which brought the fire of God. Mordecai altered the course of a nation through uncompromising intercession and holding true to his convictions despite opposition. Joseph radically changed the course of his destiny and a nation's destiny by walking in integrity day in and day out, being a great administrator, and correctly interpreting the dreams of influencers. On and on, we can talk about prophets who called out and anointed Kings behind the scenes. We have Elijah and Elisha who raised people from the dead when no one else was around, Daniel who stood for the Lord by continuing to give thanks to the Lord, and on and on. Much of the impact of the Kingdom was done outside the relaying of sermons, and messages to nations. Yes, sermons are important and much needed. But the point is for us to see what God is doing. We have to get unfocused with sermons behind church pulpits being the primary way God ministers.

So often I will be with someone, and God will be rocking him or her with a prophetic word; or I will be in an encounter with someone, and the Lord is ministering through an angel to that person. Others will be saying, "we've got to get going because we need to get to the meeting." It's then I have to say to them, "Hello, God is doing something right now." Many times, the one getting ministered to says the same thing. These kinds of moments can often be more important than anything that will go on in the next meeting because a life-changing prophetic word will be listened to many times over, processed, and declared far beyond the remembrance of the particular meeting that was attended.

Recently I was with a prophet who has been having a great impact in the Kingdom. He and I and another were in his room spending some time chatting when an angel showed up. I noticed and acknowledged the angel in the room. As soon as I did, all of us encountered the glory of God. For close to an hour, the prophetic started flowing in that room. Strategy and direction started coming to that person through the prophetic flowing out of my mouth in partnership with the angel. During this time, the prophet kept getting messages from the hosting church that it was time for coffee, then it was time for church, and also they were wondering where he was? In the midst of that, he heard the Lord say, "Stop looking at your watch, or this encounter will stop!" He then told me, "Keith, this was the whole reason I came, this is way more important than the meetings I am preaching at." He then told me that he had been seeking the Lord for a whole year for the answers that were coming in that prophetic angelic encounter.

We have got to stop getting so obsessed with doing meetings just to do meetings and start paying attention to when the Lord wants to meet. He often meets in unlikely ways through unlikely people. He is raising up unlikely carriers of his prophetic word. We as leaders and prophets need to be willing to see who and how God is releasing the breakthroughs needed if we don't want to miss out on what He is doing.

If we want to be a part of what God is doing, then we have to be willing to adjust our view of what is "ministry", where "ministry" can take place, and who can minister. Often, we are so fixated on the "right" people ministering that we are overlooking who is actually carrying the breakthrough needed. In the next chapter, I want to delve into discovering that prophets aren't "safe" to a predictable way of life, but God designed them that way. They are meant to bring the upgrade that is needed.

Chapter 3
Prophets Aren't Safe

One of the things I do is run schools to develop prophets. I am called to help prophets get healthy foundations. I am passionate to see many prophets who are known in heaven and healthy relationally get released into their realm of influence here on earth. One of the challenges of having a bunch of prophets in one room is that they all want to speak and share their opinions. Imagine having 40 – 50 Peter type personalities in one room with a few John the beloveds, and that will show you the kind of folks that are in these schools. Running prophet schools is like herding lions. It isn't natural, and it isn't easy to do. Sometimes I'm like, "Why Lord, did I on purpose put myself into this type of ministry?" I knew what I was getting into when I signed up for this assignment the Lord offered, but at times it isn't for the faint of heart.

For a while, I tried hard to keep most of the unhealthy ones from speaking. I reasoned as a leader that I didn't want them defiling the room with their bad theology, or bad attitude, etc. Then the Lord began to pry my hands loose of the controls and said, "Keith just let them go for it. Let them speak, and it will be a lot easier to train them once they are in the game speaking, even if they're making a mess, than trying to hold them down."

Prophets all think they have astounding things to say. Why? Because they have been getting revelation from heaven. They are, in fact, prophets. Their role is to hear God, and that's a good thing. The challenge is we want our churches to have the word of the Lord, but we don't want to have any messes. You can't have the prophetic released without fire. People often want the prophet without the fire. They want nice neat prophecy that is done in an exact way every time. That is not the way prophets roll. Now I am not saying prophets shouldn't be teachable. They need to be teachable and in accountable relationships. But if we are going to get the kind of breakthroughs we want in our churches, lives, cities, and nations, then we are going to have to release the mess makers.

The problem is we don't know and trust them, and we aren't going to know and trust them until we release them. How much fire could we have in our churches, meetings, and lives if we were up for a little more adventure? Shouldn't we trust that people could also spot the rotten fruit on the emerging and developing prophets? Shouldn't we trust that others could tell, just as much as we can, when someone is out of line?

Sometimes we don't want to release the unknown prophets because they are messy and untested. But Jesus set the model by releasing his apostles and even called them apostles right at the start. As they made messes and mistakes, he then dealt with those mistakes, but stayed connected to them and gave them many opportunities to grow and develop.

When we were in Fiji running our first supernatural school overseas, we sent out all the students into the villages within the first few weeks. We expressed to them, "You are now the ministry team," even though they had never prophesied or laid hands on the sick until then. They quickly found breakthrough and many people were healed, filled with joy, and prophesied over. After a couple of these outings, some of the students started strutting around full of pride in their newfound activated prophetic gifting's. The gifting's were very simple and not very profound, but they had never experienced that level of notoriety before. Only the pastors and chiefs of the villages were considered significant, and now these ministry team members were recognized as carrying something substantial. So, they quickly became prideful. “I am a prophet,” they quickly began to say. I was a bit disturbed by this until the Lord reminded me that this was good. The issues that needed to be dealt with started bubbling up to the surface so they could be addressed. It gave us an excellent opportunity to teach on how to get your identity around who God says you are and not how you move in the gifts of the Spirit. The pride was dealt with, and the people started getting healthier.

Jesus would release his disciples to minister and then call them on bad motives. When James and John tried to call down fire on a city, he quickly called them into account for the kind of evil spirit that they had released. Competitiveness rose up, and Jesus then talked about being a servant. Elitism came forth, and Jesus said to them that they needed to celebrate a variety of people, as long as they come in the name of the Lord. He didn’t eliminate his disciples from ministry but taught them along the way.

What would it be like if we decided to pastor the prophets in our midst instead of trying to keep them shut down? What might happen? So often I hear from pastors who say there are no prophets in their midst, or there are some prophetic people around, but they are scary, unhealthy and not trustworthy. Of course, many times they are right. They are all those things. They will never become anything different if we don't embrace them. God gave David the misfits as his army. The discontent, distressed, and in debt gathered to him, and he became their leader. What if we are trying so hard to keep those that God has given us under our control. We see their issues, and so we don't want to release them. What if we just started releasing them and in doing so we learned how to raise up disciples that changed the world. Yes, there will be a few more messes, but if we don't release them, then they will continue to do what they've always done; undermine.

People are meant to be heard. If they are not heard in a healthy context, they will undermine. We as leaders may blame them for gossiping or stirring up stuff against us, but the truth is our control is just as much the issue. We may call our control "wisdom" in pastoring the flock. But, in reality, it is just plain control out of fear. Fear that we will lose what we have tried so hard to build. Maybe we will lose some dignity, but in the end, we will have just like Jesus had. A set of disciples that turned the world upside down. Once yielded and developed, prophets are amazing.

Hey, I know about messes. I've made them all, or at least it's felt that way. I've ministered in the wrong way, at the wrong time, to the wrong people, in the wrong spirit, and sometimes with the right word. I've had messes that have taken years to clean up. I've reduced churches to a much smaller number. I've hurt people with the sword that cut off their ear instead of healing their heart. But I've learned. I've had some great mentors that have spoken the hard things into me and have helped me see that my heart was right but my methods needed changing. Sometimes my heart wasn't right and needed to be adjusted. But as I've been extended grace, so I've become much more sensitive to what God wants to release, what is the right amount of Heaven to bring in, and what I should and shouldn't do. I've learned that I'm not here to please man, but I am here to honor the Lord and help build the church and the Kingdom and not tear it down. It's not always easy, but it's worth it.

Yes, prophets are often not very safe, and they can be messy, but they are worth investing in. We must be a part of changing the dynamic of the rarity of healthy prophets and go after seeing prophets get healthy. Yes, there are many prophets out there waiting to be seen. But they are not going to come forth and get healthy without courageous leaders and pastors who give place for them.

In the next chapter, I want to deal with the lie that says there are no prophets in the church. I've heard it said from leaders, and people alike, and it isn't the truth. They may not be in the package we expect them to be in, but they are amongst us. Maybe one of them is you!

Chapter 4
There Are No Prophets In My Church, Are there?

Often, I will share that there are prophets amongst us to a local pastor or a leader in a church. I will tell him or her that I am looking to raise up a company of prophets in his or her area from their church and a few other churches. It will then be that I hear the reply… "There are no prophets in my church." I will say, "Ah, but yes there are. That person is a prophet, and that other person there sure has the potential, but they just aren't that healthy."

Why don't we recognize the prophets amongst us? It is because they are often in seed form. The prophets amongst us often aren't that healthy, they have already made many messes, they are hurt, rejected, speaking at the wrong times, too intense, angry, bitter, you name it. We have to change that negative perspective about prophets. It's interesting that we want to see a move of God, but we don't want the prophets. In the Old Testament, we hear that God doesn't do anything without revealing himself first to His prophets. That is still true for today. Prophets are often forerunners. They see and hear things before others do.

I remember in my first church I had two prophetic people that were both different prophet types. One was a seer and another a prophetic intercessor. They had both experienced the move of the presence of the Holy Spirit and were ruined. One of them went through a season of his whole family misunderstanding him. The other started sending me books about the move of God that was on the earth. At the time, I was a slow to receive pastor who didn't perceive what God was doing. My two church folks kept feeding me with information on the move of God and had to take my continued disagreement with them until God showed up and visited me. It was then that I thanked them profusely for staying in there until my hardheaded nature changed so that I could receive what God was pouring out on the earth.

You see, prophets and strongly prophetic people are in our congregations. They perceive and know things that God is doing, or is about to do. Sometimes they also perceive what the enemy is doing. The problem is they, at times, don't have a healthy model for how to get the word of the Lord to those that need to hear it. I've seen it all in my day. Prophets that stand up in the middle of a sermon and tell off the pastor and the congregation and then leave the building.

I used to have one of those in my church. A prophetic man and his daughters would come to the church, and they would stand up and prophesy in the middle of the worship or sermon and then proceed to disappear before I could get to them to talk to them after the service. I began to try to create a little protocol saying hey we want to hear the prophetic word but let's first get to know you. I think this is great protocol. Prophets need to be accountable for the words they give. So, we as leaders must develop the protocol for this to happen. Now we can't create the protocol that shuts it all down, we need to have a protocol that encourages the prophetic word of the Lord in the church meetings. We know the church meeting is not the only outlet for the word, but we still need to make room for it there. It is important in the meeting if it is done right.

I've had times when I've been one of the bad tempered (grumpy) prophets who feels ignored and overlooked, and I get how hard it is for a prophet in a local church to keep a good attitude under that. Pastors often don't want to release the prophets in the church because they are scary, unhealthy, and often unteachable. Prophets have to learn to be teachable while pastors over congregations have to learn to train, while also continuing to give a place for growing messy prophets to come forth. It's not easy, but if we want a move of God, we first have to let the prophets be released.

Often, when I hear a pastor say there are no prophets among them, I have to begin to show that pastor who the prophets are. I'll say, "That person is a prophet there, and that one has the potential." The challenge is when the prophets are in seed form they are not recognized or ready. You see, there is a difference between the calling of the prophet and the office of the prophet. Samuel was called at the age of twelve to be a prophet indirectly. It was the first time he heard the word of the Lord. But after that the Lord let none of his words fall to the ground, and his word began to be recognized in all of Israel that he was indeed a prophet. Historians say it took him twenty-two years between that calling and when his word finally came to all Israel. That's a long time for Samuel to be ready to be a national prophet. But God knew that he had to be prepared and ready. David was fifteen or so when he was called to be King. But then it was another fifteen years or so until he was given the Kingship over Judah and another seven years after that until he was given the Kingship over Israel. During that process, he was running for his life from the present King and his brothers didn't believe him even though they saw him anointed as King by the national prophet Samuel. There is a distance between when someone is called to be a prophet to when they are received as a prophet. The distance is the training. We as leaders need to be able to perceive the potential in someone and help put them in a growth process until they begin to get healthy and ready to be heard.

Now there may be many prophets right in your midst with a variety of gifting types. Some may be seers, intercessors, musicians, and teachers, or any combination thereof; but they are all valuable and all needed. In the next chapter, I want to talk about not disqualifying some because they don't fit our view of what a prophet should look like.

Chapter 5
They Certainly Don't Look Like a Prophet

Recently I was in a meeting with a highly-anointed signs and wonders prophet. I enjoyed his ministry and was getting some time to take him around for a few meals and asked him about his five-fold call. I asked him if he felt he had a calling as an apostle, prophet, evangelist, pastor, or teacher. He said to his knowledge he had none of those five callings. I went away and thought about it for a while and then came back to him and told him that I though he was a prophet, but after the order of Moses or Elisha in the form of a demonstration prophet.

He had never heard a prophet described in that form before. After hearing me, he said, "You know, you may be right. I had just always disqualified myself because I didn't fit into the typical type of a prophet." He was thinking of a certain prophet type that he didn't fit the mold for and so he had disqualified himself. We spent several hours after that talking about the different types of prophets in the Bible, and I was able to unpack for him the importance of his prophet type and knowing that he is a prophet.

You see, if someone is called as a prophet but is not recognized as a prophet, both personally and by others, their potential to bring impact and change in that call won't be fully realized. This is not about that person needing to be famous and called prophet for the sake of prestige. If we don't recognize and receive those that are prophets amongst us or in ourselves, then we won't see the power of that identity released.

I remember some years ago when I first came to The Mission church in Vacaville. The title of "prophet" was undoubtedly revered in my world and certainly not something you would declare over yourself. It was a rare commodity and reserved only for the few that were larger than life or at a distance from where we lived. I joined a church that had a few prophets in it already, and they were definitely on my pedestal.

Our staff had been going through a season of everyone developing an identity statement from their personal prophetic words and then presenting that identity statement to the rest of the staff. The whole goal of preparing these identity statements was so that we could begin to relate to each other according to how God saw that person rather than just seeing each other as normal and ordinary. We wanted to see the greatness in each of us because God is in each of us. The more we agreed with the greatness of God in our lives, the more those characteristics would be able to be released and impact people for God's glory.

Well, that week it was my time to declare my identity statement. I had spent time preparing my five-sentence identity statement with the help of several other staff members who had helped me go through several significant prophetic words to pull out the identities God was declaring over me in those words. One of the identities was that I was a prophet. The night before I was typing out my identity statement, but had kept the identity off the page with the prophet language in it. I grew up in a denomination that believed in prophets and apostles, but they were not anyone we knew and nothing you could ever hope to become. If God called you to be a prophet, you were a rare commodity. Well here I was with an identity of a prophet, and it seemed God wanted to call that part of me forth. I certainly wasn't going to declare that out in front of the staff. Not only that, but there were several well-known prophets in staff, and I thought how can I declare myself as one amongst such great prophets as these.

That night, God gave me a dream. In that dream, a prophet friend of mine told me that if I did not declare I was a prophet to the staff, then I would not be able to cash in on what that identity declared. In the dream, the prophet identity had to be declared to cash the spiritual check. Once declared, all the "value" or "money" attached to that declaration would be released. Then the Lord gave me a random verse when I woke up from the dream. When I looked up the verse, it was about being a prophet after the order of Elisha. I knew God was speaking, but it didn't make my day at staff any easier. I went to staff and was called up to share my identity. I read out my identity statement and included the part in there where I declared I was a prophet. But I didn't do it with authority or confidence. Instead, I did it with fear and trembling. After I was done, one of the leaders said, "Keith, it sounds like we are torturing you by having you read this statement. Could you declare your identity statement out again like you really mean it?" (I really appreciate that our team has called me up over and over again in my identity until I believe what they and the Lord sees in me.) I then proceeded to declare out my identity statement again. I'm not sure how much more confident I sounded then, but I guess it was enough to get by.

You see, God was after me beginning to receive myself in the way He saw me. Having God call me a prophet and others start to see me that way was not my idea, but His. Having to declare I was a prophet was hard and something unacceptable in my upbringing, so this was a revolutionary battle for me.

Often, we have a hard time receiving others or ourselves as a prophet because we compare ourselves to someone else. We imagine that all prophets are supposed to thunder the word of the Lord with great boldness. We think that prophets are fierce looking and don't smile, and when they release the word of the Lord, everyone bows in holy repentance and submission to what was spoken. We imagine a true prophet looking like Elijah bent on taking out Jezebel, or Daniel boldly standing up for what he believed in despite opposition. We think I could never be someone like that, or there certainly aren't any prophets of that caliber around here.

God began to take me through a journey where He told me He wanted me to study up on all the prophets in the Bible. He wanted me to do this so that I could spot the many different kinds of prophets that are out there and call them out. In my studies, I discovered there are close to eighty named prophets in the Bible, as well as hundreds of others that were a part of companies of prophets. Many of those prophets were extremely different than each other. Some never preached a sermon; others' primary way of communicating the word of the Lord was through a prophetic act. Some were known for prophetic intercession or worship. Several prophets were only noted to minister to one man, a King or an influencer. I began to see the many different varieties of prophets that are out there.

I am surprised when I go into churches and movements that have embraced the prophetic gift and even prophets from the platform. Often, I will see so many prophets amongst the people in those places, but they are unrecognized, walking around with such untapped potential. They are in a culture that declares there are prophets, but that culture doesn't create a pathway for the prophets within it to discover and fully realize their unique prophet calling. Now I by no means am declaring that I have figured out the totality of that pathway, but I am on the journey of trying to find it. One of the ways I am doing it is by doing what the Lord asked me to do. Point out the prophets amongst us and help them see what kind of a prophet they are.

Why is it that we have no problem calling anybody that runs a church a pastor no matter how small the church is or how unhealthy the pastor is, but we won't dare to declare that someone is a prophet until they are famous, or look like a powerful prophetic voice. There are many prophets among us that are not going to "look" powerful. They are mighty, but their personality may be much more tender and gentle. They may be primarily meant for intercession, and so their prophet call doesn't manifest through them looking like a teaching prophet.

Yes, I know that all new covenant prophets are a part of the five-fold mandate to equip the saints. Ephesians 4:11-12 says,

> "It was he who gave some to be prophets, some to be evangelists, and some to be pastors and teachers, to prepare God's people for works of service, so that the body of Christ may be built up."

But equipping can look like a variety of things, and we need to expand what we think a valid expression of equipping is. The problem is we often connect equipping with how teachers equip. We say that for some to be considered an equipper, they need to be able to teach line by line or communicate clearly. I know enough prophets to know that some of them speak in riddles, parables, or are generally not great communicators. They have something important that needs to be heard, but it takes a skillful interpreter to figure it out. I'm not saying that prophets shouldn't work on communicating clearly. I liked seeing Bob Jones who went on to be with the Lord in 2014 often speaking with an interpreter, and not for the sake of being understood in another country. The interpreter would be another prophet who would interview him, ask him questions, and then help explain to others what Bob was saying. I liked that we weren't disqualifying Bob because he wasn't always speaking in an easy way to be understood.

Now often I'll be talking to a developing seer prophet, and they'll be speaking in symbolic language that I can't understand. I'll stop them and say can you please tell me that again in a way that I can understand. I am surprised by how clear they then become. I know prophets can be clearer and often with the help and the proper questions, the needed clarity can be drawn out. It can be hard on a prophet who sees so clearly in their head what they are sharing, but when they speak it, nobody seems to get what they are saying.

Often prophets are seeing something that is not yet revealed to others, and endure the stigma of being misunderstood and feeling rejected until people catch up to what they saw. I know that we can change that in the body of Christ if we would simply begin to value the different ways prophets speak and not be impatient with them when they don't seem to make much sense. We can teach them and help them begin to communicate in a way that is understood by many. I notice that sometimes prophets speak in riddles because they are trying not to confront an issue that needs addressing. They have learned that speaking directly to a situation is often not well received and so they then mask what they are saying in riddles. Other times it is wisdom to speak in parables.

I noticed this in my own life as I started developing my prophetic call. I would want to speak something to someone, but as I began to speak it, I noticed they did not receive my direct communication. So, I learned how to pray what I wanted to say into that person. When I prayed it, they received it. Then I began to learn that sometimes I could pray something, sometimes I could prophesy something, and sometimes I could say something. Other times I could ask questions that provoked thought rather than gave answers. I had to learn when to use which tool. Sometimes I couldn't even pray into a person, but rather had to pray it to God and let God deal with it.

You see, it's not easy being prophetic. It's not that you picked the prophetic call. The prophetic call was chosen by God for you. But it still doesn't mean you don't go through the bruises and pain of saying things at the wrong times and in the wrong ways that people don't want to hear. We don't know what we don't know, and often learn the hard way that the prophetic word is often not appreciated or valued because it is coming through the package of us. I believe prophets can get healthy and can learn to say things in the right time and in the right way. I believe prophets don't always have to speak what they see and know. They have to begin to understand their metron and know who and where they're called to speak. Just because you see something doesn't mean you should speak it. Paul said that he was an apostle to the Gentiles and Peter to the Jews.

> Galatians 2:7-8, "On the contrary, they saw that I had been entrusted with the task of preaching the gospel to the Gentiles, just as Peter had been to the Jews. For God, who was at work in the minister of Peter as an apostle to the Jews, was also at work in my ministry as an apostle to the Gentiles."

It didn't mean that they couldn't speak to the other ethnicities, but it helped them understand that their main place of influence was in a particular field of people.

As prophetic people, we have to ask ourselves are we called to minister in a particular place and if so, how are we received there? What are the tools of bringing influence there supposed to be? Like Samuel, has our word now been recognized by the people we are called to minister to? It took him a long time until his word finally came to all Israel. He may have carried some things he wanted to say, but it wasn't yet time for them to be heard by all.

I want you to embrace that there are prophets among us in our congregations, and even in our families. But prophets are often without honor in their hometowns and amongst their own families. God will most often start off a prophet in those settings to teach them how to minister without honor so that they can handle a ministry with honor. Once a prophet can learn to not live with a rejection complex or continual feelings of being misheard or unheard, then God can entrust him or her with the influence he has called them to have.

I hope you are beginning to get a bigger lens for the prophetic people around you and wanting to see them get healthy and whole. In the next chapter, I want to talk about how prophets need to be trained rather than kicked out of our midst because of the messes they make.

Chapter 6
Can That Person Be A Prophet Even Though They're Not Healthy?

A prophet is just like any other person. They don't come in perfect form, and they are often around us daily or weekly; we just don't recognize them yet. We love to hear the special speaker that travels in from another land or watch the powerful prophetic voice through the internet. We think to ourselves, "oh to have such prophetic people around me Lord, would you send me someone." God has most likely already sent you prophets, but they are in rough form. They may be your spouse or child, or staff member, or even a church member with a turbulent past.

If you look at the prophets in the Bible, you will see they weren't the best at fitting into the cultural norm. How many of you would like to have an Elijah around or a John the Baptist? They certainly did not dress very trendy, and John ate things that most healthy eaters wouldn't eat. Nevertheless, we love to talk about them in our sermons and Bible studies. Now I am not saying that prophets shouldn't learn to be able to adapt to society and learn to speak in ways that are understandable and receivable. New

Testament prophets need to be in community and in healthy accountability. You can't just barge into a city, church, and government and sound the gong declaring that God will judge the evils of that situation. That is not the way God primarily speaks anymore. We can't use the prophet models in the Bible as excuses for our bad relationship skills as prophets. We have to take the time to get healthy and learn to speak in ways that can be tested and talked through rather than just coming into a situation and declaring out statements that are nonnegotiable. New Covenant prophets see differently and have a different responsibility than the Old Testament prophets did. They see in part and know in part, and the part they do see comes through the imperfect and developing personality of a New Covenant believer.

The goal in all of this is to begin to create pathways for prophets in training to get healthy rather than benching them or setting them aside because they are messy. I like to refer to certain prophet types at times as having the personality and characteristics of Apostle Peter. (This is not the only personality type of a prophet, however.) They are strong, can often stick their foot in their mouths by saying the wrong thing at the wrong time or the right thing at the wrong time. But they need to be heard because without Peter, we would have no Acts chapter two harvest or shadows healing many people. Without Peter, we wouldn't have anybody besides Jesus walking on water. We desperately need Peters. (We will refer to current day Peter-like prophets as "Peters.") They are often the first to step into something new, and they are the first to say something, possibly the wrong thing, that maybe others were thinking but would never say. So, Peters have to go through a journey of learning when to say what.

I remember early on in my prophet training, I would go to a church and declare out that there was an elder brother spirit in that church or something of that nature. The pastor would ask me who it was and I would tell him who I thought It was. He would then have me get on the phone and tell that person that they carried that elder brother spirit. Of course, that didn't bring life and encouragement but rather suspicion and turmoil to the church. It then took me two to three years to clean up that mess and rebuild trust with that congregation. I had to learn that just because I saw something did not mean I had to declare it out immediately. Sometimes I could see something but God was starting to teach me to speak in hiddenness to what I wanted to see grow instead of speaking it out to other people. He started asking me what is the right spirit to be released rather than focusing on what was already wrong in the church.

Another time, I remember going to a church and the pastoral team had met with me to talk through what I saw for them as a team and as a church. Well, the instant I arrived, I saw that the pastor and his wife needed to make a change. I thought they should leave the church to make room for those that were coming. I also thought they needed to step into the next season of their ministry. That thought would not leave me the whole time. So, when I was asked by the team to speak, I could think of nothing else to say. I had already been talking to the pastor about the word I was hearing, and he was resonating with it, but had not talked to his wife about it. So, when I was asked by the team to speak, I didn't share that, but shared other observations. They could tell I had more in me that needed to be shared and continued to chide me to speak everything that I saw and hold nothing back. Eventually, I gave in and told them that I saw their pastors leaving. Well, that was like throwing a grenade into the meeting. Boom! Things blew up, and not in a good way. The pastor's wife was devastated, and their team was distressed. I then had to be driven by the pastor's wife to the airport the next day. Needless to say, it was a very awkward conversation with me saying sorry many times for what I said.

Later, I found out that some other prophets had been speaking around the same issues to them for several years, but no one had been as direct as I was. I had sensed a season change in their midst, but that wasn't the right way to share it. It didn't leave room for the team to judge the word, process it, or create pathways to the changes needed. They were forced to either receive or reject my words. Dismissing a prophet's words can set people up for failure. If you as the leader reject the word, the people can think you have missed the Lord and can come against you. If you reject the individual as a prophet, then you are making a statement to the people that you don't receive that person as a prophet. This dichotomy, in turn, can cause the people to no longer trust your ability to bring in the right people either. It's a lose-lose situation.

I learned from that lesson that I don't have to say everything I feel in the moment. I have experienced that if I hold onto things of that nature until later, I will most often feel the burden lift to speak. I've also learned that I can only speak to the measure that I have relational trust built.

I remember another situation where a pastor was having a problem with a staff member. He invited me to speak into this individual and shared how grateful he would be if I did so. I wanted to help the pastor and thought it would be great to get this win. How good would this reflect on me if I could get a breakthrough in the staff member where the pastor couldn't? Wouldn't I be considered a hero? Yeah, right. It never works out how we think it is going to.

So, I proceeded to speak into the staff member. What I found was that this person had some valid hurts that they needed to work out with the pastor. I couldn't just fix the staff member. I needed to send the staff member back to the pastor to have them work out their differences. So that is what I suggested. Well, the staff member didn't just go and work things out with the pastor, they went and told the pastor off. They told the pastor all the things he had done wrong and totally devastated the pastor. This person was the pastor's potential successor.

Instead of bringing reconciliation between the pastor and the staff member there was now an even greater hurt between them as well as a not so bright future for that relationship. Of course, who do you think was blamed for everything? Of course, you guessed it, the visiting prophet. For two years, every time I tried to call the pastor, I would get ignored. Whenever I was in the same room with him, he was cold hearted towards me. I didn't realize what was going on until one day the pastor finally set up a lunch meeting with me and told me what happened. He then asked if I had set up his staff member to blast him with words of accusation. I said to him of course not, I would never do that, and I wanted them to reconcile. But the staff member had taken my words of needing to have a healthy conversation as ammunition to unleash all their venom on the pastor. Thankfully, the pastor and I reconciled after that.

As you can see, I continued to learn that just because I see something doesn't mean I should say it. Just because I am asked to speak into something doesn't mean I need to or have enough relational strength to do so in a way that brings fruit. I have since learned to use more wisdom in whom I speak into and when I speak into them.

A prophet should not be written off just because they make messes at times. Of course, they are going to make messes. A Peter-like prophet is going to make messes until they finally learn to yield the forerunner gift to Jesus and learn when to break new ground, when to speak, when not to speak, when to act and when not to act. Once Peter yields, then he becomes a force that releases a mighty harvest, opens up a brand-new people group to the gospel through Cornelius, has his shadow healing people and has the anointing to break out of jail cells. But it took three years with Jesus and some heavy duty humbling to get Peter ready for full leadership. That never kept Jesus from coaching him, rebuking him, loving him, walking with him, and continually inviting Peter into greater encounters with himself. Jesus had to be healthy himself to not hold a grudge against Peter for betraying him and denying him. Jesus had to believe in Peter enough to restore him and give him another chance.

If we are going to see the harvests we want to see, the breakthroughs into new people groups, places, kingdom expansion and increased supernatural, then we have to be willing to restore the Peters that are messy and do things the wrong way. We must be quick to forgive but also willing to keep confronting in love until the messy Peters become yielded Peters. We don't want to break Peter of his strength but merely teach him how to offer his strength up to accountable relationships and the Holy Spirit. We desperately need the prophetic Peters that God has put in our midst. But leading them also forces us to have to deal with our insecurities.

Whether you are a Peter or have Peters in your midst, you should know that it takes greater courage to have a Peter around. Peters have gotten a lot of bad rap, but what I have learned since I am a Peter, is that Peters have huge hearts. Peters are quick to repent and have huge sensitive hearts that are moldable. Peters may seem so powerful and strong but underneath they are often broken, rejected and wounded. They are very tender and sensitive to words rightly or wrongly spoken to them. I have personally improperly handled Peters, and it cost me tremendously. When Peters are treated wrong, they can internally grow a root of bitterness. That bitterness is devastating once Peter starts to share it with others, usually through venting frustrations. That bitterness spoken out can cause many people to rally with them on the journey of destroying a church, leader, or even a movement.

Peters may seem to be the strongest in the bunch yet when they are cared for, called out, believed in, and confronted in love, they are loyal and will give you so much more than they have taken in their mistakes. They are worth loving into health. We must stop writing off the prophetic Peters amongst us because of our hurts from them, and must embrace greater wisdom in dealing with them so they don't destroy what we are building, but instead become a valuable part of developing what is going to be built.

In the next chapter, I want to talk about not only embracing the Peters but also learning to see that God has designed there to be many prophets and high-level prophetic people amongst us. God is restoring the lost companies of prophets to those who are ready to accept them. There may be many unhealthy prophets we are not willing to receive as prophets amongst us, but for those that say yes to the task of embracing a prophetic company, the rewards are immeasurable.

Chapter 7
There Can't Be That Many Prophets Around Here Can There?

For so long, prophets have been put on such an unhealthy pedestal that several extremes have arisen because of that. Here are a few:

1. The complete absence of prophets amongst us.
2. An overly powerful prophet in a church or organization.
3. Unhealthy and unteachable renegade prophets hanging out on the fringes or the outsides of our churches.

If we are going to bring health and a restoration of many prophets among and around us we have to be willing to embrace that there are many different types of prophets with various levels of influence. Just as much as we would have no problem deeming a pastor of a church of twenty congregants a legitimate Ephesians four pastor, so also we need to begin to see that there can be prophets that have a very small metron as well.

When I started out in my prophetic development, I was pastoring a church of around one hundred people (on a good day) in a town of six thousand people. As I developed my prophetic calling, I began to develop friendships with the city manager, regional pastors, and a few leaders in other nations. Although my local influence seemed small, I was still having a significant impact for the size of the area I lived. Another prophet rebuked me for saying I was just a small-town pastor with little influence. He said, "Keith, you could be having the most influence of anyone in your area. Look at all that you are impacting on a larger level. Maybe you don't see the hundreds come through your church doors, but that doesn't mean you don't have a much bigger impact." It was evident that I needed a perspective change.

Just think about one of King David's personal prophets, Nathan. The primary prophetic ministry we see him functioning in through the scriptures is to one man, King David. Even though he ministered to this one person, his influence ultimately affected nations. I have an incredible personal intercessor that has the caliber of a Bob Jones at the level that he sees in the spirit on my behalf. He can take out the demonic realm when it attacks me. He is also able to help me understand the purposes of the angels that God releases to help me. I don't care where I am in the world. If I call him and say help, he almost always has extremely helpful insights and something in the spirit realm shifts to bring a breakthrough on my behalf. I am so thankful for the personal Nathan the Lord has given me. His impact is touching the nations in partnership with me.

Of course, he could feel like, "What is my impact?" He works a local job that is just average in his eyes and feels bored and constrained at times to doing the great things he knows he is called to do. I have to remind him that his impact is so much bigger than he can imagine and the victories I get are his victories too.

We have to begin to realign our understanding of Kingdom impact and what being a prophet really means. If we start to see that there are a lot more prophets among us and even make room for the possibility, then we will be surprised by what we get.

Whatever you make room for, you get. I love going to churches where there are vast open doors and a place for strong local prophetic voices to speak. One church I went to surprised me with the great prophetic words that were released on Sunday morning. I asked the Lord why was I even needed there? They had already done such a good job. Of course, there is always a purpose for an outside perspective, like mine, but I was still discovering it.

Whatever you value you get. When I pastored, I began to attract a bunch of prophetic folks. Of course, when they arise from a place of hiding, you see their unhealthiness, and the glamor is quickly over. They need help and healing; and at first, they are going to take their hurts out on you if you are their leader. When that begins to happen, it is our tendency to want to shut down the prophets and not give them room. One of them may want to conduct a strange prophetic act in front of everyone, another chooses to blow the shofar, another desires to dance, and another aspires to prophesy in riddles. How do you pastor that? It takes a special grace to create pathways for prophets to flush out their gift or else they will bottle up and begin to release their prophetic authority against you. That is not pleasant. You can love everyone, but I have learned you can't release people into a position of influence if they are unteachable. I have to first get them to a place of being loved, and trusting, so that then they'll let their guards down and learn to be teachable so they can get healed and whole and become useful for the kingdom.

I find that whatever you make room for in your heart, you attract. For years, it was the heart cry of Heather, my wife, and I to have spiritual fathers. God gave us many. Some famous and others not famous by man but famous in heaven. I learned to attract fathers by painting a sign on my chest that said, “good soil.” Fathers love to speak into me because I am a learner and receive the inheritance that they give whether our connection is a long-term connection or a short one. In the same way, wherever I go I receive lots of encouraging words and prophecies. I have two whole notebooks full of amazing prophetic words plus other files and mp3’s of many small prophetic snippets people have spoken over me. I value the prophetic word, and just as much as I give out the prophetic word, I cherish receiving the prophetic word. Whatever you make room for, you certainly do attract.

As I have started to raise up schools to develop prophets, I see many different types of people come out of the woodwork that are prophets. They come in all shapes, sizes, and levels of health. Whatever you begin to see, you begin to attract. I see and believe in prophets, and so I attract them. Some of them are looking to be loved on, some are already amazing in their calling, and some don't even know they are a prophet yet.

One of the points that I encourage in my schools is that if you are highly prophetic, just come to my school whether you think you are a prophet or not. I share that because we have not had a framework and a pathway to get prophets healthy and recognize there are prophets amongst us, we may have already disqualified ourselves from being a prophet. Watching some students for months I have noticed that some don't look like prophets to me, but as the school progresses along, suddenly, I will see it. Wow, there is a prophet in that one. Look, there it is. It's unhealthy, it's in baby form, it needs to be nurtured and trained, but there it is. I've been surprised a few times.

Leaders and even you may be surprised at the prophets around you. You may even be one yourself, much to your astonishment, as you begin to embrace the journey to explore the possibilities. Even if you come out on the other side realizing you or others around you aren't an Ephesians four prophet, the discovery process will be ideal for you. It will settle in your heart your identity in who you are and also who you're not. If you're not a prophet, it is not a disqualifier from being amazingly fruitful and significant. God made you the way He thought you would be the happiest. Embracing who you are and who you are not is a place of great fruitfulness. It shouldn't be a shame.

I see people so often try to become a pastor, or step into a position as a prophet because it is in their eyes the only place of esteem. They are miserable, and the anointing of the Lord is not flowing and can't flow with them when they are declaring they are something they are not. Only when you are fully embracing who you really are, is there actual lasting fruit.

Even more so, if you are a prophet, you need to embrace it. Prophet will be at a deeper core level of who you are than being a worship leader, intercessor, teacher, etc. If you are a five-fold prophet, then you need to flush that out and get healthy in it. This is mainly because the prophet is a significant identity that defines what you do and the impact you will make. Yes, we do have an even greater identity than that as a prophet; we are sons, friends, and the bride of the Lord. But when you are a prophet, it is not primarily about what you do and whether you prophesy or not, but it is about who you are. It is a place to rest. When you are a healthy prophet, you are a demonstration of who Christ is in His nature as a prophet.

Let us begin to believe that there are many more prophets around us and amongst us than we realized. Yes, they may be in raw and unhealthy form; but just like a baby, we don't throw the baby out with the bathwater. We develop the baby until the baby becomes healthy and whole. Some emerging prophets may be closer to being a healthy prophet than you think. Others may take a little longer, but that's the joy of the journey.

In the next chapter, I want to talk about having a whole bunch of prophets in one place. It's a concept that has been around for thousands of years in the Bible, but it is not something we see too often today. It's time to change the rarity of companies of prophets. Bringing them back will restore the presence of God to greater levels.

Chapter 8
Is It Possible To Have A Bunch of Prophets In One Place For Very Long?

Getting a group of prophets in the same room together and learning how to really value each other is sooooo challenging. Did I say soooo? Yes, I did. If it were easy, we'd already have companies of prophets in our midst. I see two different situations when I go into certain churches. Either they have no prophets at all, or they think they have many prophets. They like to say, "Oh yes, we've been training prophets for years."

Of course, that'd be great if it was real. The problem is that in most places, I've seen people say they have a bunch of prophets in their midst, but it's not usually a real healthy environment.

One of the goals I shoot for in my prophet training classes is that we're not just looking for prophetic people in our midst; we're also looking for New Covenant prophetic people in our midst. Thus, we must really define the New Covenant. I believe God is not going to be releasing high-level prophets that are carrying a mixture of both covenants. We have a lot of mixture in the prophets that have been raised up over the last thirty years. I know we would not be where we are today without them, but we need a few upgrades for this next wave.

Prophets carry such weight, so they need to make sure their theology; their eschatology, their character, their gifting, and their foundations are healthy. One of the signs of a healthy prophet is that they are in a community, they are known by local people, and everything in their lives is in the light with someone. There is nothing hidden. For so long, prophets have felt so alone or even live alone, and they need to be with others. I see several of the famous prophets of our day travel a lot and have no healthy base where people truly know them. That model must change. How can there be companies of prophets if there is not a consistent gathering together?

Often, I hear about certain prophetic roundtables and how wonderful they are. I know some are great but some seem to have a lack of relationship at the core. Usually, you will see or hear about a group of prophets gathering together and discussing what is coming, what is God saying, etc. But how can that be a community of prophets when most of the time everyone is trying to share their latest and greatest revelation? Then the next prophet must share a more profound revelation. To me, that doesn't feel like the highest form of community.

God wants to raise up prophet communities. Out of those, prophetic roundtables will come. Revelation flows so much better when there is deep trust between one another. It is hard for prophets to trust one another. It takes a long time. Why don't prophets trust? (I put myself in that mix as well.) It's because we are too often using the "gift" of suspicion. We call the "gift" discernment, but it is just a lack of trust in God's ability to put good in others. That is why it has been difficult in the last 50 years to establish healthy sustainable prophet communities. There hasn't yet been a wineskin conducive to handling it. The wineskin needed to manage it has healthy mutual relational honor flowing in it. If we are to see companies of fifty prophets here and there established within a regional context, we need first to have trust built. Trust takes time.

I know this about myself - that I am slow to trust. I am getting better at it, but I realize that often when I have a new connection with someone, I am initially a bit distrusting. Or if I'm not distrusting, I'm not thoroughly enjoying myself and relaxed. It takes work to build relationships with others. Often when I go to a new church, or into a new relationship, I know the first time together may not be the best. We're still checking each other out. I may have some great things to prophesy or an excellent atmosphere to bring, and that really takes down some walls, but still our conversations outside the context of a great meeting are almost like swords jousting. We are wrestling with each other's beliefs and ways of doing things. As a prophet, when I come into a church, I can't help but see what needs to be adjusted or what is wrong or missing. I must work at ruling my gift and not letting what I see cause me to mistrust people. I must realize that no one is perfect and things are just going to take the time to build trust so that I could even be a part of the solution to some of the issues seen. On the other hand, I may not be called to be a part of solving those matters anyways.

These are all challenges for a prophet in getting to really know and find a cohesive connection with other people. How much more is it challenging for prophets to find great connections with other prophets? Thankfully I have seen it become possible and am learning how to have other prophets as friends.

At times, you will see a group of prophets that are gathered and overseen by one strong senior prophet. They may call it a roundtable, but in reality, often it is a pyramid because the senior prophet carries all the weight. We don't often see a community of healthy prophets that still maintain lines of leadership, but isn't top heavy, or competitive.

Sometimes when I get around prophets, revivalists, apostles, or reformers that are similar in gifting or age as I, often I can feel a competitive edge to the gatherings. I have fought hard to not engage in the elder brother spirit in those settings and relationships. The elder brother spirit inhibits brotherly connections from happening. It's a bit like the tall poppy syndrome seen in Australia or other places. That syndrome is described like this: when someone rises up in gifting or favor, the rest of the people below bring that person back down to the ground because nobody can get too far above anyone else. We see it in Scripture with Cain and Abel, Joseph with his brothers, David with his brothers, and even Jesus and his brothers. There is an inability to sincerely value the favor and gifting on others because there is a fear that if another brother or sister gets more favor than me, then I will not have the favor for what I am called to do. The lie that perpetuates that spirit is that there isn't enough blessing to go around for all of us.

I have had to learn to beat down that spirit in my life by celebrating the brothers and peers that carry a similar anointing or favor as I. Whenever I feel that edge of comparison, I just start celebrating that brother or sister and asking them about all the amazing things going on in their life. I won't exchange war stories of victories God has given in my life at that moment. That brings out the competitiveness. I honor and value them until that person settles down in their insecurity. Usually by the end of our time together, there is a great connection happening between that person and me because they feel valued and unthreatened by me. We may eventually become great friends and do some wonderful things together in the Spirit. But that won't happen until that spirit that divides and prevents trust is broken down.

There must be an intentionality to honor and value one another to build prophet communities, even if there are similar gifting's. Real fathers can help create a culture that allows one another to value each other. If there aren't true fathers in the midst, then there is insecurity, and insecurity doesn't breed true unity.

God wants there to be companies of prophets. As a solid team of Mission Vacaville leaders including myself has fought for prophet community in my home base in Vacaville, California, I have noticed that as months of gathering together in schools, or in homes goes on; there slowly begins to be a trust that forms. Breakthrough starts happening when people start celebrating and even sounding the praises of another prophet. When the different emerging prophets begin to receive from one another instead of one up each other in a ministry context, then unity starts to happen. There is such a power when we can seamlessly flow towards one greater purpose while each of our individual purposes are still intact and useful in the greater context. Once people stop trying to only think about how they are going to advance their personal ministry alone and begin to think about promoting the greater purpose, then heaven shows up.

We have seen many great individual prophet ministries with one main voice, but we don't often see companies of prophets or even several prophets and apostles flowing together for extended periods of time. I love to minister with other prophets. I have one spiritual father who has been a prophet for over thirty years that whenever we get to minister together, it is so powerful. There is a seamless but complimentary flow back and forth, and often one will speak or prophesy, and the other will confirm what was shared. This is a great joy. I love team prophesying. There is one thing to prophesy with other prophetic gifted people, but it is entirely another thing to prophesy with other prophets. When there is security in everyone's hearts and identities, then there is no need to be the biggest voice or most profound. There is simply a joyful flowing back and forth until what God wants to release has been flushed out.

I believe we are going to begin to see companies, groups, and pairs of prophetic voices emerging that are secure with each other, powerful, and enjoying and celebrating one another. We see that whenever companies of prophets flowed together in the Bible, enemies of God were confused, overturned, and demolished. Samuel, Elijah and Elisha had companies in the Old Testament. Agabus was a part of companies in the New Testament. Of course, there were also the dynamic duos of Silas and Judas, Barnabas and Paul, Paul and Silas, Peter and John and others. Whenever they operated together, there was a powerful release of the Kingdom. When Paul and Barnabas split up, there was a significant loss. It is challenging for strong prophets as well as prophets and apostles to flow together. It takes the foundations of trust, and healthy relational skills built. That is why up until today, we haven't seen many powerful duos flowing together or companies of prophets. But I believe it is time.

There has been over twenty years of the Father's love released since the Father's blessing was initially poured out in Toronto in 1994. That began to change our view of relationships, fathers, and the heavenly Father. It began to create inroads to change our wineskins so that we didn't have such a top-heavy hierarchical model. When that started to happen, healthy teams came to the surface. We are still fighting for those healthy dynamics to fully emerge, but we are starting to see where churches, leadership teams, and prophetic companies are operating in the Father's love. Building upon the Father's love, while functioning in mutual respect and honor for one another and leaders, we are seeing a shift begin to happen.

I still believe God appoints leaders, but I think our view of leadership is changing. Some are still holding onto a very top heavy view of leadership, but that will never release a truly healthy prophetic community. You can't have healthy relationships that are fully vulnerable and at times messy when there is a strong leader at the top that ultimately shuts things down if things don't feel right to him. His or her ability to control the environment, even a Kingdom environment, won't allow the messes out that need to be seen. It is hard to keep prophets in check, but I am learning that I am not supposed to. I am called to release a safety where the frustrations, failures, disappointments and successes can be heard. It is easier to manage those when they are out in the open and not kept in check. But an insecure leader won't allow frustration or disagreement to be heard. We will never see true prophet communities without the changing of hierarchy structures.

In the next chapter, I want to talk about this changing in our view of leadership so that there can then be an emergence of the prophet companies and Kingdom duos that are so needed.

Chapter 9
Where Are The Prophet And Apostle Teams?

You can't have true teams of prophets and apostles emerging that model the Kingdom until there is mutual trust between the two gifting's. Of course, we need five-fold teams emerging as well, but I want to focus on prophets and apostles primarily in this chapter.

I have found that over the years, whenever I get with an apostle where we have mutual respect, we begin to experience an acceleration in the Kingdom together. I find that when I am with an apostle, or even when operating as an apostle and I am with a prophet, the Kingdom advances.

I have been with apostles just enjoying a meal together, but suddenly, we are together leading the waitress to the Lord. At other times, I have seen healing beginning to flow where we go. This is different than me coming in as a special speaker at a church gathering and seeing healing or salvations in the meeting. I have witnessed these harvest moments happen time and time again with a variety of different apostles and prophets that I connect with, so I know that God is showing me something.

God designed prophets and apostles to flow together from early on. In the Old Testament, there was Moses and Aaron. When they flowed together and communicated properly, blessing flowed. When Aaron felt unheard and started to back talk Moses, then the enemy took over. I learned that if I have a person on a pedestal in my heart, whether they are a spiritual father or a spiritual brother with a larger influence than me, then I am often unable to flow with them. I can flow in the Spirit in a meeting they are doing, but it is separate from what they are bringing.

One of two things need to happen. I have to take them off my pedestal and learn to relate to them as a peer, or I need to recognize that this is a valuable relationship but may not be a synergetic one. Synergy flows out of mutual trust. God wants to change our views of Him, and in that, we have to see one another differently. For so long we have been under the Father Son dispensation. But that view of God and us often puts God at such a higher level than us that we find the goal of our relationship with him is obedience instead of a partnership. Now don't get me wrong, God is still the King of Kings, the only way to heaven, and much greater than I in every way. But there is a paradox in this. God doesn't want just to be the biggest person in the room. He is so secure in who He is, and He has offered us more than a relationship with Him that is a servant to master relationship. He says in John 15:15, "I no longer call you servants, because a servant does not know his master's business. Instead, I have called you friends, for everything that I learned from my Father I have made known to you."

That is such a beautiful mystery to me. When I have learned to honor Him as King, then He can entrust Himself to me as a friend. Friend means there is a mutual dialogue going on. I like how Abraham operated in his friendship with the Lord. He was considered a friend of God but still had tremendous respect for God. We see it in the story of his intercession over Sodom and Gomorrah. Lord, even though you are big, pardon me for asking, but will you not destroy these cities if there are righteous people in the midst of these places? He barters with God while maintaining respect. We need to learn how to negotiate with God, but from a position of respect.

Our cultures have taught us to disrespect rules and authority figures under the guise of personal freedom. I disagree with the spirit that comes out of that wrong view. I do agree that there must be a freedom we begin to walk in with one another if we are going to see heaven invade earth in increased measures. I have noticed that some of my relationships with spiritual Fathers and Mothers in my life have changed as I have begun to see them as something other than just great wisdom and input that is needed in my life. As I began to realize that I am valuable in the relationship and have something to say as well, then things started to change. I have also had to change how I handle our relationship. Instead of continually relating to them and drawing on the wisdom side of their gifting, I have had to start nurturing the friendship aspect of the relationship as well.

Now, of course, there are some people that for a variety of reasons will not allow me to relate to them as a friend. I have to be okay with that and can still choose to receive their fatherly input. That will keep our relationship in a Father-son mode and may limit what I can do in the Kingdom with them. But, for those that are willing to see a change in the relationship and begin to change with the adjustment, there is potential for another kind of relationship.

It is much like parenting. There are seasons when I am mainly father to my kids. But there comes a time when I begin to realize if I don't adapt to their need to be heard more, to discuss issues that we need to deal with, instead of me just telling them what to do, then we are going to get stuck in our relationship. They may get bitter at my inability to have dialogue and then push away from me relationally. As a father, I need to be able to see the necessary transition in our relationship and navigate it accordingly if I want to continue to grow in how we relate. There are times I can still pull the father card out and may need to, but it is much rarer. Personally, I enjoy the dialogue with my kids, and as they have begun to move more into having their views, I have at times received adjustments in my character as they point something out in my life that needs changing.

I have been enjoying this relationship with my biological father, Mark. Recently after living apart for twenty years due to jobs in different regions, my dad and mom have moved into the same city as me. I had wondered before it happened how things would be. Would we still relate to each other out of past views of father-son relationships? Surprisingly, we have, without saying much about it, renegotiated our relationship together. It is much more like friends or peers than as a father and son. I still ask Dad and Mom for advice, and at times they are a needed voice of wisdom, but on other occasions, I have advice for them. I am still going to honor them as father and mother, but I am finding a new joy and a synergy in our lives, as I am not merely trying to obey my Father and Mother's advice.

If we are going to have kingdom apostles and prophets flowing together, there is going to have to be a similar shift in how we view each other relationally. If one person feels they are the apostle in the relationship and thus the one that must be listened to at all costs, then there will be an inability to partner together. Partnerships in the Kingdom are much like marriages. In an old wineskin view of marriage, the husband is the head, and the wife is in a subordinate role. Now scripture doesn't change, but our view of scripture does. In my early years, the husband being the head meant it was my job to hear from God for the big decisions in our life, and her job to support and trust. In the old view, it is always the man's task to provide and the woman's task to nurture the children and run the household.

Now I know that this is not now operating in most of the western world, but I use it as a simple illustration of the changes that have come.

Now I have come to understand that whenever we make decisions together as husband and wife, I need my wife's wisdom and insight. Sometimes I am going to defer to her and trust her even if I don't personally quite get what she is seeing or feeling about a particular situation. I know now that not listening to her under the guise of being the "head" of the household is going to hurt me. My wife wants to feel safe and protected and cared for around me, so I still have an important role as the "head" of the household. The way that "headship" is flushed out looks different than before. There is still respect flowing to me, but there is respect flowing from me to her as well. I like it so much better.

Our view of God is much the same transition that we are making. Whenever we change our view of God, or He reveals another side of His nature, a whole new way of relating ensues. When that shift in the relationship comes, we experience an enlarging of our capacity to receive other blessings and perks that that new side of God reveals. When we enter a friendship with God, we then come to a place in our relationship with Him in which He wants to give us whatever we ask. He trusts us and then takes it on Himself to bring about our dreams. John 15:16, "You did not choose me, but I chose you and appointed you to go and bear fruit—fruit that will last. Then the Father will give you whatever you ask in my name."

That is the same flow that will happen when apostles and prophets get comfortable in their differing yet important roles. When we are not competing for who is in charge, then we will begin to see an increased harvest together. Wouldn't it be great to find the prophets and the apostles that are around you, that may or may not be famous, but are powerful and influential in the kingdom? What could happen if we looked for those strategic relationships instead of trying to hold onto our authority, position and gift as the main gift that is needed? What could happen if we started reaching out in our congregations and pulling up people that don't see themselves as important as us? What if we were secure enough in our positions that we could bring not just one, or two, but many into a place of carrying a voice and an influence in our world? What could happen? It takes wisdom and courage to do that, but it is so needed.

I have seen pastors empower team to be the apostolic or prophetic company only to find it end in disaster. Why? Because they put a title on the group too fast and didn't allow the relationships to grow organically. This is not about calling someone your prophet, or apostle, or a part of your new team. That is a very practical way of doing things. Why not try building trusting relationships over time first without putting any titles or roles on anybody? It's better to see how people respond, and then nurture and at times adjust the relationships according to what comes out when increased trust or ministry opportunities are given.

I worked with one pastor who raised up several "Apostolic" teams too quickly, and those teams tried to take over his job. They even moved into wanting him to present his sermons to them for approval, and so forth. Those teams didn't last long and resulted in that church having some significant fallout and people leaving offended. It was a good concept but wasn't built with the wisdom needed in the situation. When people haven't had a voice for a long time, and many prophets haven't, and they finally get a voice, it is like giving the microphone to a person that never gets the microphone. One or two things happen. The anointing doesn't come out because the person is too nervous, afraid, or self-conscious. The other thing is the person over speaks and loses any opportunity of speaking again because everyone didn't enjoy that experience. It is a bit like when someone hasn't received any attention, and then you give him or her some, and after that, they want to hang out with you all the time. You're like whoa buddy, let's take this slowly. If they keep pushing in, you may push them away. It takes a secure, gentle, and gracious person or fatherly or motherly person to walk that person through the process of learning how to be sensitive in how much they should say or not say and when to speak and when not to.

We as leaders must be willing to allow time and continued opportunities in safe environments to flush out the prophetic voices we need in our midst. They will need regular feedback, encouraging, and adjusting if they will ever get to be healthy. We can't expect to have great team dynamics when we don't give the team time to develop and build trust. Much like I was sharing in an earlier chapter about my slowness to warm up relationally, although I am getting much quicker, we must allow team trust and ministry together to grow.

I ministered with one of my mentors/peers in this last season together on a Sunday morning. I was the one that suggested we partner together. Now I have partnered with other prophets and apostles in a tag team approach in meetings and have seen great success. But this time it wasn't so great. We both had in our minds how we thought this meeting would flow. The problem we quickly realized is that we each build on the platform a different way. One wasn't better than the other, just different. It took a little while to talk that through and get our hearts feeling great about each other after that. It felt like a few steps back in our trust to do ministry together, but after we had adjusted, we moved forward together again. This time in another ministry setting he ministered and then invited me to minister in a particular area. I also ministered and then invited him to minister in a specific way. In this way, we were then drawing out the differences in a positive and timely way that worked together beautifully. We have several more trips planned together, and as we grow together, we are each finding our roles. I love what Joel 2:7-8 says about the army of God,

> "They charge like warriors; they scale walls like soldiers. They all march in line, not swerving from their course. They do not jostle each other; each marches straight ahead."

In a healthy Kingdom team, there is an ability to move forward in the things of the kingdom without jostling each other. Each in their own distinct and important role, but alongside each other in the same army. We have seen for years what one powerful ministry can do. We have also seen for years what one powerful ministry with many workers can do. What would happen when there are several key leaders working together in a variety of initiatives in the gathered church and scattered church as well as in the marketplace and society? What would we see accomplished when we begin to value diversity while operating under similar values? There must be similar values if we are going to function together. How can two walk together unless there is agreement, the scripture says.

In the next chapter, I want to talk about the need to have different prophetic voices in our midst if we are going to move forward. Navigating and understanding how that flushes out is the key to seeing what we can't see on our own.

Chapter 10
Why Do We Need Other Prophetic Perspectives In Our Midst?

When you open up the door for many different voices to be heard, you are asking for an initial torrent of confusion, misunderstanding, and mess to potentially come to the surface. It is so good and needed, but also needs to be understood.

Trying to hold forty to fifty prophetic voices in check was a task I was attempting in one of my schools. I had worked for months to make sure only the healthy voices were heard. The problem was there were very few that I deemed healthy. Most of the other voices had little glitches in their theology, character, or views in general. I didn't want that to "taint" the class. Finally, one day with a smaller group of students that had been with me for over a year, I accidently let the cat out of the bag, so to speak. What followed was not expected. I opened our time together with the smaller group of ten to fifteen students with a question that resulted in a discussion of politics. That's a loaded subject. My goal in doing so wasn't to try to leverage everyone eventually over to my side, but to use the issue of politics as an excellent opportunity for people to recognize that as a prophetic voice, we can't speak and prophesy out of our personal political views. We must prophesy from heaven's view with the Kingdom in mind and must discern the difference between heaven's view of politics and our personal views. They are more different for some of us than we realize.

What ensued from that conversation was initially a bit of mayhem and what felt like anarchy. Only a few students that have been friends and with me for years knew the greater goal I was trying to achieve in allowing this conversation to happen. They knew I was attempting to train the students in how to identify the difference in personal opinion and a Kingdom viewpoint. I'm trying to raise up healthy prophets that don't use their sphere of influence as a place to leverage for their personal agenda.

But what seemed like a spiraling out of control meeting was a God setup. I had been feeling the increased difficulty and the greater and unwanted tendency to want to control every moment of the sessions I was leading. This was God's way of changing my view on how to lead the team towards healthiness. As people started to share, or should I say vent, their opinions, more and more passion came forth. Tears started flowing, and voices started getting louder. A few even momentarily stormed out of the room. I was thinking to myself, "What is happening here? Did I miss something? Do I need to bring things back into order?" No, I needed to give them the opportunity to let their frustrations come out. What resulted was that some people felt voiceless and others felt like they weren't getting the attention and input they needed from fathers, namely me. As it flooded out, some individuals felt awful that there was such emotion coming out of them. It wasn't a pretty conversation, but a necessary one.

It took a while, and we didn't get it all cleaned up that day, but what resulted was people getting some personal revelation of their unhealthy expectations, their pent-up frustrations, and some needs they had. To the best of my ability, I tried to help people see that their unmet expectations weren't all about me falling short in caring for them, but in their inability to become powerful in solving their problems. Yes, I could grow and develop a better culture to help meet some of those needs, but at the end of the day, prophets have got to take responsibility for getting their needs met and for learning to let their voices out in a healthy way.

Later, I was so glad that their voices had finally come out and I resolved not to work so hard to keep everything managed so well. I decided I could be a bit more like Jesus who released His disciples to do ministry even when they had a lot of character still to develop. In the journey of ministering and letting their voices out, Jesus could then adjust their pride, competitiveness, judgmental tendencies, and other wrong views. To choose to hear other perspectives and let the voice of the bride and the prophets be heard, we must be willing to speak the truth to one another, preceded by grace, wrapped in love. This is one of the core values of my home base at The Mission.

It is refreshing to hear the different and many voices that are in the body. I love hearing others' testimonies, perspectives, and encounters with God, other people, and general struggles in life. The body needs to be heard, and the prophets are a big part of that. Much of what we hear in church often primarily comes from the "polished" voices. Polished is only a matter of perspective. Often, we use the words "weird" or "immature" for other voices we would rather not hear in a public setting. But I have come to realize that "weird" is most often used as a label from someone that is uncomfortable with a different kind of voice or perspective. My calling you weird is me saying you don't look like my normal. Of course, we all think we are normal and everyone else is weird, or we believe everyone is normal, and we are weird. Either way, we need the "weird" voices to be heard. Of course, I am not talking about the dangerously unhealthy voices, and the obvious voices that are carrying pollution, bitterness, and impurity in their hearts.

Early on in ministry, I did not receive anyone outside my "normal spirituality box." I thought the way I encountered God was the superior way to encounter God. For me, it was speaking in tongues, fasting and praying, and being bold for Jesus by preaching and evangelizing on the streets. That was the radical and "superior" way. Anyone else not operating in my way was less than me and possibly not even saved. I'm being a bit facetious, but I'm probably not far away from how I felt back then. God had to begin to adjust my thinking by bringing people into my world that didn't think, act, or minister in the same way I was used to. I began to hear different definitions of what it meant to be full of the Spirit and flowing in the Spirit and what the presence of God was to them. Of course, I didn't receive those views very easily at first. But as time went on, God began to bring me into encounters that I would have never had if I had stayed in my narrow way of seeing Kingdom expression flushed out.

One prophet God introduced to me, against my will, has become a life-long mentor and trusted influence in my life. Twenty years ago, when I was at a meeting, a lady asked me if I wanted prophetic ministry. I responded, "yes, from anybody but that bald headed and loud man." (He was ministering prophetically to some people in a ministry line). It was like she didn't even hear me and went over and out of everyone there, chose him just for me. He came over and started prophesying over me in a powerful, but different way than I was used to. He was loud, and would occasionally hit my chest, like football players exchanging respect would do. He even blew on my stomach for the sake of releasing something "spiritual." As awkward and challenging as that first encounter was with that man, unbelievably, he became a significant trainer in my development as a prophet. That night I had my first angelic encounter in my room and woke up in the middle of the night with a wind blowing in my room, and I started prophesying. I had never done that before, and my wife woke up and exclaimed, "You're prophesying." God had opened up another dimension of the spirit realm to me through a prophetic voice I wouldn't have readily received.

Over the course of the years, he has been a fantastic, and necessary life-giving and different perspective to me. He has taught me much about the Kingdom, the spiritual realms, and about victorious spiritual warfare. I would have missed a huge blessing if by God's grace I hadn't received what I didn't want to receive. God knew that I needed different perspectives and voices in my life if I was to advance and begin to enlarge my tent pegs and see what was possible in the Kingdom. For several years, God brought a variety of different voices into my life as He was dismantling my narrow mindedness. I have come to a much greater appreciation and desire to embrace a diversity of voices, and perspectives, as well as ministry styles. One thing God told me in that journey of getting free of small-minded thinking, was the ministry methods and styles of different people weren't sacred, rather the message was. I needed to learn to appreciate the different voices and the way those voices flushed out.

Some prophets are loud, some quiet, some are very poetic, others are mysterious, others are serious, and others very joyful. Some prophetic voices are passionate only about change in the government; others are excited about revival. Others continually sound the gong for intercession, fasting, and sacrifice. Some speak about morality issues, while others talk about the goodness of God. Some prophets preach with signs and wonders following, others do their best work in private and behind the scenes in counseling. Every expression, style, and way of ministering is needed.

If we are to get where we need to go and gain acceleration in the Body of Christ, in the church, and in leadership, we must learn to embrace those who are different than us. Like I said, "different" or "weird" is only in the eyes of the one who always hangs out with the same kinds of like-minded people. I travel to a variety of churches with diverse demographics. In some churches, people are all wearing trendy clothes, in other places, it's more mountainous, and thus a whole different style of clothing is worn. Neither is better, and the flavor is refreshing. But I have to adjust how I receive them and not disqualify them because they don't dress, talk, or look the same as my style of dress.

I was very much against the prophetic person that manifested by shaking, laughing, or manifesting physically. It hadn't happened to me. For several years after coming into the outpouring that was released on the earth in the 90's, I would be prayed for in a meeting. Hundreds would fall out in the Spirit while I would remain as stiff as a board. I was critical of what was going on because it didn't fit my grid for normal spirituality. But God was slowly transforming my heart; He was wearing me down with his love and goodness, and eventually, my hard heart began to feel His presence. On one occasion in front of a whole group of ministers that were also not in favor of ecstatic encounters and prophets, I was thrown to the ground at an altar call. I had no one lay hands on me, and I hadn't ever experienced this kind of encounter up to that point. I was slain in the Spirit, but when I hit the ground, I started to shout "hooo" and "woooo." After that, when I prayed or prophesied, frequently my head would shake from side to side violently. Others that could see in the Spirit would see a lightning coming from heaven through me to the person or group of people I was ministering to. This was not my idea, and I had been against those kinds of "weird" people. Now I was one of them.

For a season, people would ask me what the shaking was all about when it happened. I was a bit defensive, and at times unable to explain what was going on. The only thing I knew was when it happened, heaven would show up in greater measure, and people would be healed and touched by God's power. I have since stopped resisting God flowing through me this way.

I have occasionally had people invite me to speak in their church but ask that I cater my manifestations and not operate in them. I have had to tell them that they probably shouldn't have me come then. I am not at the place of wanting to hinder them because I notice that when I do, nothing seems to happen substantially in the Spirit through me.

The church and leaders have got to be willing to let God be God and to embrace the variety of prophetic styles and voices that are emerging and are already present on the earth and amongst us. I am not excusing immaturity and weirdness for the sake of making a scene. I am saying we are going to have to give greater room for the variety of ways God moves. He is God, and we are not, and for some reason, He continually put His prophetic word in scripture in unique individuals. Some wore interesting clothing, several were not polished, others were considered fools, others wept, some cried and some walked around in sackcloth or even naked (not normal for today). But God's word came forth.

Yes, I know we need maturity and everything decently and in order. But are we the ones determining that or are we really allowing God to determine that? When Paul told the Corinthian church everything must be done decently, and in order, it was because there was already such spiritual activity going on that it needed to be managed properly. Until we get significant spiritual activity in our church where the gifts are flowing, and the presence of God is moving through His people, then we don't have the right to misapply that verse into every situation we want to look like what a "normal" meeting is for us.

We pray for revival and reformation but then don't embrace the messy and different voices God has already put in our congregations. Yes, they have spoken out at the wrong times and in the wrong ways. Sometimes the prophetic acts they want to release aren't timely or easily received. That is why those who lead are called "pastors." We need to pastor and not eliminate prophets and the different ways they manifest and bring His Kingdom.

So many people want the prophets, but they want them in a nice teaching style and wonder why we don't see the fire of God's presence falling on us. If we would begin to let go of control, stop categorizing people as "weird," recognize that our normal is not the only way, then we will see much more begin to happen.

Yes, it is going to take courage; it certainly has for me. In choosing to train prophets, I had an idea of the cost. I counted the cost. I knew that I was choosing to have the strongest, sometimes obnoxious, or hardheaded, weird and unusual people come into my midst. That was going to take courage. But if we are going to see a different day, then we are going to have to be willing to pastor those voices until they become healthy and heard. It is a great adventure and one filled with rewards, if chosen. In the next chapter, I want to talk about just that, learning to embrace and pastor the prophets amongst us.

Chapter 11
How Do I Start Finding And Embracing Potential Prophets?

If I am going to have prophets in my midst, then, first of all, I am going to have to believe that there are indeed prophets in my midst. I've shared it before, but often; I get to a church and ask a pastor if there are any prophets in their church. He will say not in my church. I also have asked church leaders of the prophets in my current schools, and they'll say I didn't know there were any prophets in the area. The reason they respond this way is because they hold a stereotypical view that a prophet should be a thundering Elijah type personality, that is bigger than life, and shatters a nation with their words. I'm thankful for those voices, but there are many other kinds as well.

For so long, prophets have been received as they were in the passage of scripture in 2 Kings 9:11,

> "When Jehu went out to his fellow officers, one of them asked him, 'Is everything all right? Why did this madman come to you?' 'You know the man and the sort of things he says,' Jehu replied."

Funny eh, but not too far off the truth. We often refer to the prophets among us as madmen. Unhealthy, weird, unusual in their prophetic mannerisms and prophetic acts. Yes, they are at times all of those things, but if we are going to see an army of needed prophets raise up amongst us, we have to be willing to receive them in their present state and then choose to start pastoring them towards health.

The very reason I have started prophet schools is to get prophets healthy. That is the whole goal. Train them so that they can be palatable, sensitive, and free of rejection, in community, vulnerable, loving, gentle, and kind.

How do you start finding the prophets amongst you? Look for the people around you that have an unusual gift of prophetic sight. They see things in the Spirit, they are always prone to give prophetic words, or they always want to tell you what the Lord is showing them. Look also for those who are prone to do prophetic acts, prophetic intercession, want to flow prophetically in worship, have a prophetic word for your church or the people around you, etc.

They may be unhealthy or imperfect in the way they operate in these gifts. You may not want to see them as a prophet because they may be your spouse, or even yourself. But they need to be embraced. You can't tell if someone is a prophet while they are in training. Sometimes you can, but often I won't even see it until someone gets in their metron of influence. Sometimes when I hear a person preach, suddenly, I will think yes, they are a prophet. The difficulty I have had with them is that they are unhealthy in their character and so I haven't given them any place in my heart as a prophet. But as soon as I see the gifting in its right context, then I know that they are. They just have a lot of growth to develop in until they are ready to be fully received.

You see, we can't write people off because they're messy. If you are in church leadership, one of your jobs is to create pathways for people to get to their destiny. Prophets need pathways. Where are those pathways? Do we have them in most of our churches? No, we don't. That is why we have unhealthy prophets. We haven't even given them a place to flush out their calling. They need to be around other prophets. They need to have the opportunity to get around healthy prophets and seasoned prophetic voices. They need to have a company of other prophets they can relate to.

If you are their pastor, you need to affirm that they have a prophetic call. You don't have to release them entirely, but they need to have hope that there is potential for them. They need to see a way through. That is why I have created the online training sessions to develop prophets as well as books, workbooks, and schools for prophets. I want to give them pathways wherever they are so they can feel hope.

My dream is to have hundreds of prophet companies all over the world who are community-based, connected to the church, having training sessions that accelerate their development, and providing places for them to flush out their calling.

How do I start finding and embracing potential prophets? I must value them enough to create opportunities for them to develop. If I don't have opportunities for them in my church or leadership scope, then I need to be willing to send them to get trained or help connect them to a pathway of development.

I also need to be ready to hear the prophetic people when they are processing. Sometimes talking to prophetic people is like speaking to someone from a foreign country that has very broken English. I am always asking them to repeat themselves, explain themselves, and I have to listen very carefully to understand what they are trying to say at times. Prophetic people need to be shown grace. If you show them grace and treat them with dignity, even if they are eccentric or a bit unhealthy, you will be surprised by the gems you find that come out of them as they get healthier.

It is hard work having a bunch of prophets around. I have the battle scars to prove it. They say things the wrong way, sting you with their words, speak kindly one moment and the next moment hammer you with their frustrations. But if God said that prophets were needed to raise the church up to her place of glory, then we must be willing to be a part of getting prophets healthy.

In the next chapter, I want to talk about how to begin to embrace the fact that you could possibly be a prophet. Sometimes we can see glimmers of a prophet in others, but other times we have a hard time recognizing it in ourselves.

Chapter 12
Embrace The Fact That You Could Be A Prophet

Whether you are a leader of a church, or a congregant, a businessman, or a housewife, you need to be willing to embrace that you could potentially be a prophet. What you do for a living, or what you spend your days doing, doesn't determine whether you are a prophet or not. Prophets come in all different forms and shapes. Just look through the Bible. You will see prophets in many different varieties. They appear as male and female, young and old, wealthy and poor, in leadership and working a regular day job. Some worked with royalty and others were very unpolished. Each carried a distinct purpose and need for the Kingdom of God to expand their sphere of influence.

So often, we qualify or disqualify ourselves from being a prophet because we are looking at how people receive us. Do we have a platform in the church? If not, we don't have much hope that we could be a prophet. Maybe we have a platform in the church, but it is not the one we feel is conducive to being a prophet. We must get this pattern of thinking out of our minds. It's not constructive to think that all prophets need the pulpit, or need to be received at a high level from a personally preferred church that we deem important to be considered a successful prophet. This wrong thinking could not be further from the truth.

God may have called you to primarily be a prophet to the marketplace or even to individual leaders. Your primary call may never lead you to be in front of large crowds, but for some of you, it will. The main goal is to not look at the present circumstances you are in to determine if you are a prophet or not. God often raises up prophets in their hometowns or places where they are seen as little Susie or quiet Bobby. People may not see you as a great leader or as a prophet, but that doesn't mean you aren't. On the other hand, I have seen people try to force on others that they are a prophet, and that isn't the right way either. A person's gift will make room for them Proverbs 18:16 says,

> "A gift opens the way for the giver and ushers him into the presence of the great."

Likewise, if you don't embrace that you could be a prophet, the calling of the prophet could lie dormant within you for a lifetime. Matthew 22:14 says, "Many are called but few are chosen." Many are called by God to walk in the office of prophet, but few choose to go through the development to make themselves a vessel worthy of honor. Paul says in 1 Timothy 1:18-19,

> "My son, I give you this instruction in keeping with the prophecies once made about you, so that by following them you may fight the good fight, holding on to faith and a good conscience. Some have rejected these and so have shipwrecked their faith."

Many have forsaken their prophetic words and so have shipwrecked their faith. This leads me to believe that just because you are called to be a prophet doesn't guarantee that you will step into the fullness of that office.

I have seen many reluctant prophets in my time. They are like Jonah. God has given them an assignment, but they are resistant to it. They don't feel qualified. They don't feel ready. They have experienced rejection, or they don't want to go where God has assigned them. Jonah had an incredible harvest once he submitted to God's assignment. Sadly, however, he never got in alignment with God's heart for the people of Nineveh.

You must be willing to embrace the assignment with joy. Recently, I was with a seer prophet who hadn't embraced his calling to be a seer. He has amazing angelic encounters, and whenever he shares them, he experiences huge favor. Leaders of movements want to partner with him. But he had resisted, for years, until by God's grace he finally listened. The moment he said yes to the favor and assignment of his seer call, then doors flung open for him within a couple of days. They had always been there, but he hadn't deemed himself worthy of them. He didn't want to be bothered by the people that would want his attention.

It is true that there can be, at times, notoriety for being a prophet. When people see the gift that we operate in, they often want to take advantage of it. They don't realize what they are doing because they are just so hungry for the secrets you have found in God. If we don't learn how to have healthy boundaries, then we will get bitter and shut down our gift towards the people we are called to serve and equip.

The Lord had to take me through a several-year process of teaching me how to maintain healthy boundaries. People can at times try to pigeonhole you into a specific role as a prophet. For me, at times it has been the joy boy, the man of fire, the prophetic word machine, and the prophetic psalmist. Whatever way you manifest the presence of God, people will often want to keep you in that vein. Now it is good to recognize what Kingdom keys we have and be willing to serve and train the body in those. The key is not just to use those gifts. If you are a prophet, you are called to equip the saints to walk in the gifts you carry. Often, people don't feel they could ever operate in that and just want to get another word from you. That is a cheap way of looking at a prophet.

Sometimes we watch how a word of knowledge prophet operates and are mesmerized by their gift. They develop a great ministry out of moving in that gift, but in reality, they are called to equip the saints until the place they operate from becomes the new standard for the body of Christ. Often, we want to keep them on a pedestal instead of taking responsibility to learn ourselves.

I've said it before but for years I have had the privilege to have an amazing seer prophet by my side. He is amazing in taking out the demonic attacks that come at me or unleashing the angelic help that God assigns to me. Over the last year, I have begun to ask him how he does what he does. At first, it seemed utterly impossible for me to operate as he does. But as time has gone on, I have little by little begun to gain confidence in being able to spot the angelic and partner with them as well as identify and take out the demonic. That is how a prophet should operate. He should equip others in what he does so naturally.

I also have the grace to attract business guys. They like me, and I like them. God has put a divine connection between certain business leaders and myself. We mutually enjoy each other's company, and I find that because we usually have a desire to expand the Kingdom, as well as their business, we work well together. Usually what naturally happens in those relationships is that, in a healthy way, I provide them with prophetic insight and at some point, they tend to want to sow into me. There aren't any strings attached on either end to do that, but it just naturally seems to happen. Now, keep in mind, I'm also not saying there haven't been times when strings were attached. But that's found in my book, "Unlocking an abundant Mindset."

As I continued in the relationships with the business guys, I started to realize that I needed to think on a higher level. I didn't just want to receive from them the generosity that they gave to me; I wanted to learn to think like a businessperson. I also thought, I don't want them to need my prophetic gift forever; I want to teach them how to hear God better for themselves. To me, doing things this way seems to bring the relationship to a different level. I like connecting people directly to God without them needing to go through me.

Sometimes it seems so cheap that people want to get a prophetic word or a laying on of hands from me. I will ask them, why go to me when you can go directly to the source yourself? You are going to have a much better, and in the long run, a more sustainable lifestyle with God that way.

Learning how to be healthy with your prophetic gift is key to the longevity of that gift. In the next chapter, I want to focus on a few ways to recognize if someone, even yourself, is a prophet.

Chapter 13
How Do I Know If Someone (Including Yourself) Is A Prophet?

So how do you know if you are a prophet? I have covered a few chapters defining how not to disqualify yourself or others from being a prophet. I have also described the different types of prophets that are out there. Now I want to delineate some of the clearer signs that can reflect that you are a prophet. There can be exceptions to what I am going to share, and I don't want to lump everyone in the same basket, but I do want to share a few tendencies of some prophets.

What is one of the obvious signs that you could be a prophet? It's a deep one, wait for it. You love the prophetic. Yes, I know that sounds crazy, but you can't be a prophet and not love the prophetic. I'm not judging, but just noticed that certain famous prophets I have seen no longer prophesy. That's one detail that Dan McCollam and I decided years ago not to do. We noticed that the more prophets got a name, the more they moved into the preaching side of things instead of staying in the prophetic realm. We decided that we always wanted to be able to serve the body with the prophetic gift and not just move to the teaching side.

If you are a prophet, you ought to love the prophetic word. You should love hearing from the Lord. You ought to love listening to others' stories about hearing from the Lord. If you are a prophet, you will have a hunger to know about the prophetic and the prophets. You should spend time and money to invest in reading books and going to conferences on the prophetic and prophets. It should be something that naturally draws you. In the last chapter, I shared about reluctant prophets and those that resist the call for a variety of reasons. The healthy emerging prophet that has a call should naturally be attracted to the prophetic.

Those of you that are seers should see things in the spirit and enjoy discovering what God is saying through what you are seeing. You should also enjoy hearing other prophets talk about what they see in the Spirit. If you are a seer, you should enjoy encountering angels, God, the presence of God, and the works of the Holy Spirit.

I notice that those who have a bent towards the prophetic and are potentially a prophet are drawn to having a passion for seeing God's presence show up in meetings, on the streets, work environments, and in worship. Prophets are passionate about the presence of God and often get frustrated if the presence of God is at a low level in the room. They want to see the highest amount possible of the presence of God resident in the meetings they are a part of. I have seen prophets lose their jobs because they had a radical encounter with God and chose the encounter over the dignity of keeping a job. I am not vouching for or against losing your job; I am just revealing the level of passion they are willing to live with for the presence of God to show up that leans them towards being highly prophetic.

Prophets can be very black and white in their approach. If something is wrong, it is completely wrong. If something is right, it is completely right. That can be a great attribute as well as a detriment if a prophet doesn't know how to rule that side of their gift. You will notice someone that leans into being a prophet by the black and white thinking in his or her character. They are very passionate about everything they believe. They may be an internal or an external processor, but if you get to hear them talk, they will let you know very strongly what they feel. They are like

Peter. Passionately describing what they will and won't do for Jesus. They can be very passionate about whatever makes them come alive.

Sometimes a prophet can make a lot of messes because they don't think through the choices they make. Like Peter, they insist that Jesus has to do things a certain way. Jesus is quick to rebuke Peter when he gets out of line. Peter is a good example of a prophet in between the calling and office of prophet. When a prophet is ready for office, he like Peter has come to the end of himself and has learned how to yield his voice and emotions to God. Then God can use him as a voice to bring a harvest into the Kingdom.

Prophets are very tender and can get their feelings hurt, but they don't always appear very sensitive. People usually think prophets aren't very loving, but the truth of the matter is prophets are huge feelers. They feel very deeply and love very deeply. They also get hurt very deeply. They are huge lovers of people and God, and once healthy, are a huge benefit to those around them.

Prophets also tend to not be very good initially at relationships. Like Elijah who was called to bring restoration to family, (Malachi 4) we see that Elijah wasn't very good at relationships.

Elijah was a loner. He wasn't going to be able to finish his assignment on his own, but he was a hard guy to be around. People that disagreed with him ended up getting the fire of judgment released against them or killed. God's destiny and purpose for prophets is that they are healthy and in community relationships. With that said, one way you can tell someone leans towards being a prophet is that they love to be alone.

Being alone isn't always a bad thing because prophets like to spend a lot of time alone with God. Prophets many times need the alone space to be strengthened, and that is how they connect with God. Now I am generalizing a bit, but I think overall a prophet type has these basic tendencies. Of course, a healthy mature prophet knows just the right amount of time to be alone and the right amount to be with others. Learning that balance is a key to being a healthy New Covenant prophet.

Another way you can determine that someone may be a prophet is that people start seeing that they are one. I know that sounds simple, yet it is the truth. People, leaders, friends, family and other prophets start recognizing a health about that prophet and the gifts that they carry. Of course, the challenge can be if you are in a community of people that do not recognize local prophets or even prophets worldwide for that matter, then you are in a place where there is no recognition of your gift. But overall in the body of Christ, where there is even a small revelation of prophets, there will be a recognition that you are highly gifted in the prophetic even if they won't declare you are a prophet.

Now many are highly gifted in the prophetic that may not be prophets. Ephesians 4:11-12 tells us that prophets are a part of a group of leaders that are called to equip the saints for the work of the ministry.

> "It was he who gave some to be apostles, some to be prophets, some to be evangelists, and some to be pastors and teachers, to prepare God's people for works of service, so that the body of Christ may be built up."

So, one of the ways you can tell a prophet is moving into their office is they begin to equip people. Now equipping doesn't have to look like standing behind a pulpit and teaching necessarily, but there has to be some multiplication of who they are in the saints to consider them more than highly prophetic. Prophets who are ready for their office have learned how to multiply what they do in others. If you aren't equipping the saints, you are not a prophet according to New Testament standards.

Also, prophets in the New Testament are sharers and live from the New Covenant message. If you notice, Barnabas, Judas, and Silas in the New Testament all were prophets who shared on the finished work of Jesus. In the next chapter, I want to look at how you can tell the difference between a New and an Old Testament Prophet, as we desire to see New Covenant prophets emerge.

Chapter 14
Recognizing New Covenant Prophets Amongst Us

I grew up in a family lineage with a grandpa as a prophet. He wasn't a famous prophet, but I am convinced he was and is a prophet. He was a bit of a mixture of an Old Testament and New Testament model of a prophet, however. He had a bit of the Old Testament thinking in him because he believed and occasionally saw the people that didn't respond to his message would die. He had a bit of the New Testament in him because signs and wonders followed him. People were delivered around him, healed, and the prophetic flowed out of his love for the message of the cross touching lives around him.

Now I absolutely loved, received and learned so much from my grandpa Lewallen growing up. The people in the churches he attended wouldn't have recognized him as a prophet because there wasn't a grid for that back then. But he had different words from the Lord that he would bring to the church or individuals. I loved and honored my grandpa, so I would find myself sitting at his feet learning, and as I grew older, I frequently talked on the phone with him. He would always share with me what the Lord had told him, and the words of the Lord that had already come to pass or that were going to come to pass. He knew things like the Jabez prayer would be significant to the larger body of Christ, and then the Jabez prayer became popularized by Bruce Wilkinson. He would tell me that prophets would run the end time church. He also helped me establish a belief in God's Kingdom coming to earth rather than the denomination's views that believed we were all going to be whisked away from the earth before the earth was burned up. He was cutting edge for his time.

As I came into a greater revelation of the New Covenant, I began to recognize that part of my grandpa's theology was based out of an Old Testament paradigm of how prophets should operate. Like I said before, he believed if someone didn't receive the word of the Lord, it wouldn't be too long before they could find themselves dead. I remember once I had given a prophetic word to someone in my early twenties, calling them to serve the Lord and turn back from their backsliding. They didn't listen, and the next day I heard that they had tragically died in a car crash. Of course, that validated my belief that if you don't repent, you could die.

That was about the time I was starting to connect to some New Covenant prophets like Kris Vallotton, who shared with me that this wasn't the right spirit in operation. It was a bit like Jesus' disciples wanting to call fire down on those who resisted and Jesus having to rebuke them for operating under a wrong spirit.

As I have matured in the revelation of what a New Covenant prophet looks like, I am convinced that if we are to be a part of the prophets that God is raising up for today, we must have our theology correctly built on the New Covenant. New Covenant Prophets need to have their beliefs connected to New Covenant Apostles. I have spent over ten years receiving and growing in the theology of the finished work of Jesus through Apostles such as Georgian Banov. I have spent many hours with Georgian who has helped me understand and get a firm foundation of the goodness of Christ and His finished work.

Those who build on an Old Testament paradigm will tend to lean towards a gospel mixed in with judgments towards those who don't receive. An Old Testament prophet will warn people of sin and then when there are disasters in the land, connect that disaster to the people's rejection of the warnings. How do you know if you have a New Covenant prophet amongst you? They are preaching or talking about the goodness and mercy of Christ. They are pleading for God's justice under the New Covenant. In the New Covenant, justice is when we get what Christ deserves. In the Old Covenant, justice is when we get what our sins deserve. You can tell what system people are under by what their view of justice is. I love what Zechariah says in Zechariah 7:9, "This is what the LORD Almighty says: 'Administer true justice; show mercy and compassion to one another.'" Kingdom Justice is giving people mercy and compassion.

I often say that New Covenant prophets are known by how much joy they get from the finished work of Jesus. New Covenant prophets are joyful, they laugh, they smile, and they are gracious. Yes, their typical personalities are very intense and can be very opinionated. As they grow and become trustworthy and counted ready for the office of prophet God has for them, they will be merciful, joyful, gracious, kind, and tenderhearted. They are also often very determined and strong in personality. That is a good characteristic when it yields to the finished work of the cross. They will be individuals that go the distance and fight the good fight with joy, love, peace, forgiveness, and gentleness.

We are looking for New Covenant prophets in this day who look through the lens of mercy instead of judgment. Mercy does triumph over judgment, according to James 2:12,

> "Because judgment without mercy will be shown to anyone who has not been merciful. Mercy triumphs over judgment!"

It is our privilege and challenge at times to acquire God's heart of mercy and compassion for those who are filled with sin, darkness, and problems. Barnabas is a great New Covenant example of a prophet who fought to believe in Paul the Apostle and get him connected to the Apostles of the early church. His name means "Son of encouragement." That is the very heart of the prophet. He also fought for John Mark when Paul didn't believe in him. New Covenant prophets must learn how to fight for people to receive mercy and grace and not desire judgment for them. That is how you know a prophet is ready for greater authority.

We are under the New Covenant, and that means teachers, pastors, evangelists, apostles, and prophets should equip with this as the foundation. I distinguish New Covenant prophets from New Testament prophets such as John the Baptist. We should not follow some things about his ministry, but some things are great examples for us. One point I like to help developing prophets discover is distinguishing what can be received from the prophets of the Old Testament and what can't. We benefit from funneling everything through the cross. Some things can make it through and some cannot. We aren't to emulate all the behaviors and heart conditions of Old Covenant prophets. For example, we wouldn't want to follow the heart condition of Jonah, who wanted the people of Nineveh to suffer destruction. Even though this was Old Covenant times, God was showing that he always loved people of every tribe and tongue.

Of course, as we said before, Jesus rebuked his disciples for wanting to call down fire as Elijah did. We can therefore conclude that even though that story is in the Bible, it is not a story God wants us to emulate. Here it is in Luke 9:54-56 in the KJV,

> "And when his disciples James and John saw *this*, they said, Lord, wilt thou that we command fire to come down from heaven, and consume them, even as Elias did? But he

turned, and rebuked them, and said, Ye know not what manner of spirit ye are of. For the Son of man is not come to destroy men's lives, but to save *them*. And they went to another village."

We must learn, as developing prophets and leaders, who we are to give a greater ear to, by discerning which covenant they are operating within. A few years ago, God was teaching me this. I had the opportunity to preach at a church. I felt God wanted to deal with the subject of bitterness. So, I decided to speak on that subject. I preached on the problem with bitterness. There was one story that I shared during that message that had to do with one of the leaders of that church and myself. The problem was, I didn't finish the story, so it put that leader in a bad light in front of the people. He mentioned that to me after I had preached the message. He liked the story when it was presented accurately but pointed out that I had missed finishing it.

For whatever reason, I became so bitter over that comment he made. For close to a year, I wrestled with bitterness towards that leader and that church. Then, at the end of that year, the Lord started talking to me and told me that I was good at prophesying great things over people;

even if I saw something wrong with them, I would flip it and release an encouraging word. He then asked me why I didn't flip the negative things I saw in a congregation? Instead of pointing out bitterness, why didn't I speak to the forgiveness that people should walk in? He told me that when I preached about the bitterness or the negative spirit, I empowered that spirit. That is why I personally encountered bitterness for a year. He then told me he wanted me to preach the word again he had given me the year before. This time, He wanted me to talk about a culture of forgiveness instead of exposing bitterness. What a good, but painful lesson to learn.

That is one of the marks of a New Covenant prophet. They can redeem difficult subjects. They find the gold in the midst of the dirt. They believe in difficult and challenging people. They can call people up to being the new creations God made them to be instead of showing them how much they have fallen short. They can reveal to people the mercy of God instead of preaching about the coming judgments due to people's disobedience.

God is looking for New Covenant prophets. Whatever you speak to, you empower. If you speak to sin, you enable sin. That is the lesson of

Romans chapter 7. When you teach people not to covet, according to the law, they step into coveting. You rather should show people that they are not under the Old Covenant and now a new law lives within them, the law of the Spirit of life. They will begin to walk according to the new beliefs that they are a new creation prone to do right. Left alone, they will do the right thing and will choose to follow God because Jesus lives within them.

How exciting to see companies of New Covenant prophets rising whose primary message is all about what Jesus has done. We need thousands of those voices speaking hope to the world. In the next chapter, I want to talk about some other foundations you can recognize in New Covenant prophets.

Chapter 15
Foundations New Covenant Prophets Are Known For

I have had the privilege to be around some amazing New Covenant prophets. They have helped me immensely to escape old beliefs, judgmental views of the world, others, and myself. They have also helped me see who God truly is.

We are looking for the New Covenant prophets amongst us. How do we determine who they are? Their message is filled with hope. I remember first meeting one of my prophet mentors, Wendell McGowan. I would call him up with a dream I had just had. My interpretation was filled with fear and coming from a lens of something bad was going to happen to me. He had the amazing ability to redeem anything. He could give me hope from a dream when I would be thinking something bad was going to happen. In doing so, he broke the back of fear and foreboding that I was so used to living under.

New Covenant prophets have the ability to encourage. They know how to redeem all things. That is one of the purposes of prophets. When you see someone who is washed up and seems to be overlooked by the world, a New Covenant prophet finds purpose in him or her. Even Samuel of the Old Testament was able to discover the gold in Saul at the start. He said, "Tomorrow I will come to you and tell you everything that is in your heart." What was in Saul's heart? He had in his heart the desire to be King.

I love being around prophets who know how to redeem things. A couple of years ago I started going out to do some prophetic acts with some people from our church in Vacaville. I was astounded at how one lady was able to see all the good and could redeem things within a dark atmosphere. My tendency was to see the darkness and to get a bit afraid, or on the defense. Her posture was so peaceful and called me up to the New Covenant value of redeeming all things.

Of course, redeeming all things has nothing to do with empowering or agreeing with sin or sinful lifestyles. It simply focuses on seeing that God can turn into good what the enemy intends for evil. We as New Covenant prophets are looking for the gold amongst the dirt of the spiritual climate and humanity.

Sometimes we feel like a true prophet is someone who calls sin for what it is, sin. But actually, a true New Covenant prophet is based on the New Covenant. What a revelation. In the New Covenant, God is not counting our sins against us.

> 2 Corinthians 5:19 says, "That God was reconciling the world to himself in Christ, not counting men's sins against them. And he has committed to us the message of reconciliation."

Boom baby. That's a revelation. So how do you recognize a New Covenant prophet? It is someone who is not counting men's sins against them, but instead, is looking to release mercy and forgiveness to them. Under the Old Testament, prophets called people and nations to account for their sins. They were there to show people where they had missed the laws of God and then to threaten them with judgment if they didn't repent. I am so thankful we are not under that law system. It didn't work, and that is why God had to seek for another system; A better system. One built on better laws.

Under the New Covenant, we get what Christ deserves. Our goal as prophets is to draw people to Christ's mercy, not scare them into God's mercy out of fear of judgment or hell. New Covenant prophets aren't preaching that disasters, wars, earthquakes, tornadoes, etc. are the punishment for a culture under sin. Under the New Covenant, people are under John 3:16, " …for God so loved the world." Why would He in one moment love the world and in the next moment want to punish the world? He said in John 3:17, "For God did not send his Son into the world to condemn the world, but to save the world through him." He didn't come to condemn the world but to save the world. It's not that complicated. We are to be looking for prophets that are carrying the message of forgiveness.

If someone is sharing that they are a prophet but are prophesying disasters, or revealing that a disaster happened as proof of God's anger or people's sin, they are missing the whole point of the New Covenant. We don't get what we deserve. We get mercy, which is not getting what we deserve, but what Christ deserves.

I'm thankful that the Lord put me around healthy prophets for years because early on, and occasionally still, I need a reminder that I am to be looking for good things in people instead of being suspicious of what could be wrong with them. I've had the privilege to see prophets who aren't using their eyes to find sin but are using their spiritual eyes to discern the good in others.

Over the last few years, I have met a Barnabus type pastor/prophet who has been such a good stretch for me, and I have seen his gift in action. He goes after seeing the good in some difficult people and believes they have a useful purpose in the kingdom despite my questions in several areas of their character. He has provoked me and encouraged me that there are wonderful people out there who are prophets, but who choose to see the good with their spiritual eyes. Those kinds of prophets are so needed today.

We need to begin to wake up to whom the prophets are God wants to promote amongst us today. They may not be the ones we always agree with. But if they have love, encouragement and belief in difficult people, then we should choose to give them a voice amongst us. With so much darkness in the world around us, we need prophets who can point to the light that is emerging. The more we fix our eyes on what God is doing, the more we will see that light grow.

I have met several young and upcoming prophets in the last couple years that I would consider actual New Covenant prophets. The one thing that I love about each of their messages is they do not have a beef with the world. One of those New Covenant prophets, Shawn Bolz, has had such a tremendous impact on the church already. He has an amazing gift of the word of knowledge, but his prophet message includes not having a problem with the world. Shawn has a mindset that says if we are to impact the culture around us, we can't be known for being against them but rather for the love of God impacting them. It is a huge and powerful message he carries.

I have begun to see that message emerge with the healthy New Covenant voices that are emerging around us. They are not pushing to show what is wrong with the world, but rather how God loves her and is so gracious and patient with her. I have seen that the effects of this kind of message include a great harvest. Scripture does say in Romans 2:4 that it is the kindness of God that leads us to repentance. I am so thankful that God so loved me even when I wanted to pursue thoughts and actions outside the kingdom. He was so kind and told me He would love me no matter what. In doing so, I got free of the thoughts that were holding me back.

We are not licensing sin. Rather, we simply recognize that grace needs to be preached because true grace will free people from sin, not empower it. We need prophets who prophesy from the grace of God, not the severity of God. There are times we need to warn and discipline people. Those tools are used when we have a relationship, are called to pastor, and are called to parent and father people. We don't release those words as the standard message of the prophet but rather the normal message of someone who is raising a spiritual family and at times needs to remind them to do good, so you don't give place to the devil. When Paul corrects the Corinthians, he did so as a father to them and not with joy in his heart at sharing the message, but rather a joy that they might hear the message and turn away from the sins they were walking in.

For so long we have been mesmerized with prophets who thunder God's wrath instead of extending God's mercy. It is time we prioritize what God is prioritizing. "For God so loved the world and sent His only begotten son that whosoever believes in him should not perish but have everlasting life." John 3:16. Look for prophets that aspire to love the world not judge the world. Judgment is a part of an old dispensation. There is judgment in the New Testament. It is the Day of Judgment, not a lifestyle of judgment.

What an exciting day we are living within. A day of the love of God, a New Covenant day, a day to encourage, and a day where the Kingdom is at hand. The Kingdom of God is His righteousness given to us, bringing joy and peace into our lives. I'm so excited that I get to be a prophet that ministers from this kingdom. That I get to find permission to see God's Kingdom coming to earth and to live in heavenly places rather than primarily look for the hell that is all around us. In the next chapter, I want to look at the New Covenant prophets' mandate to bring heaven to earth.

Chapter 16
New Covenant Prophets Are Heavenly-Minded

I believe John the beloved was a New Covenant prophet as well as an apostle. Some months ago, God took me into a time of intense prayer for forty days. I had been completing a study of John the Baptist. As I was studying on him, I got a revelation that he was a revivalist prophet. I imagined him in the modern day looking like Steve Hill from the Brownsville revival or Lou Engle. A little while ago, Steve Hill died. So, while I was studying up on John the Baptist, I also watched Steve Hill's funeral to try to understand this type of anointing. As I watched the funeral service, I was hit with the revival spirit that Steve carried. He carried such a message to bring revival by calling the saints to a life of purity.

After watching the funeral, I got consumed for purity to come back to California where I live as well as the nations. I spent much of the night in prayer. That next day I was asked to lead a small part of the church service. I told them I probably shouldn't be put up there because all I could think about was revival. They said we need your voice in the meeting. (I've always appreciated that about our team. They are always so hungry for revival.) So, as I did the transition, I released the fire that I carried, it was the only thing I had to release. It went on for fifteen minutes or so and then for the sake of needing to publicly honor some military people in the house we had to transition the meeting. I was still burning with fire, and so at my wife's suggestion, I took the fire into the prayer room. For the next forty days, we prayed. After about two weeks of burning with the fire for purity to see California come back to God and for our nation and the nations to receive His purity, I started to get a bit irritated. God was doing so much in those that attended during that time, including me. He was dealing with impure motives, calling us to a higher standard, and the fear of the Lord was being restored to our hearts. That was all good, but I noticed that with this mantle, I was starting to lose love and patience for those that didn't seem to embrace this message.

Then one evening before the next prayer meeting, the Lord said, "I want you to look at John the beloved now. You have looked at John the Baptist, and now you need some of John the beloved." As I studied up on John the beloved, I realized he had the makings of a prophet as well.

But his prophetic call was different. His main task was to rest on the heart of Jesus and in doing so, get a heart for what Jesus had a heart for. John's message was all about love. Love for God resulting in love for one another. He had a powerful apostolic ministry, but was also a prophet. He was caught up into the heavens and saw the risen Christ and experienced powerful but frightening things in heaven.

As I studied up on John the beloved, I got hit with the love that he experienced. I was weeping at the love of Jesus, and out of that, I fell back in love with God. Just as much as experiencing the anointing of John the Baptist gave me a fire for purity, so the experience with John the beloved gave me the fire of love. For the next two weeks, I reveled in the love that John had found. Our prayer times were sweet and powerful. The Lord then began to talk to me about the need to see both the anointing of John the Baptist and John the Beloved merge and integrate. That one of those mantles on their own would lead to a wrong conclusion. The message of John the Baptist would tend to cause us to end up not loving the people Christ loved, and John the beloved's message without it's counterpart message would tend to cause sin to creep into the church.

Both prophets were heavenly minded, as they understood what their message was. Both had encounters with heaven. John the Baptist saw the Spirit ascending on Jesus. John the beloved ascended into heaven to see the risen Christ. New Covenant prophets have seen Christ. They have seen the ascended Christ. They are caught by a heavenly revelation, and that revelation provokes them to action.

How do you know who a New Covenant prophet is? They are captured by Jesus. They are in love with Him. John the Baptist was preparing the way for Jesus. John the beloved was walking side by side with Jesus. Both were consumed with a heavenly mandate. Both saw heaven. One went up to heaven to encounter the glories of that realm. The other stayed on earth and prepared people to be able to enter into an encounter with heaven. Both are needed. We are looking for the kinds of prophets that Jesus is revealing today. You will find these prophets consumed with passion. They want to see Jesus get His full reward. That is why they are so passionate.

Finding an impassionate prophet is rare. The prophets that aren't full of passion are the ones that are running from their assignment. Prophets are full of fire and zeal, for God's house consumes them. They want to see Jesus get the reward for His suffering. They are in love with Him and are willing to give all they have so that He can be glorified. They pour themselves out over and over again. Whether they do it through music, prophecy, prayer, preaching, one on one conversations or evangelism, one thing is sure, they are known for passion.

New Covenant prophets find their desire is to live in heavenly places and encounter the risen Lord for themselves. Many of them spend hours loving on Jesus, and whenever Jesus shows up in the room, they are fully engaged. Some are aware of the angelic and are sensitive to the Spirits moving. Their main task is to see how much of heaven they can get on earth. They live to please the Father. They get such joy in seeing heaven pleased.

Healthy prophets have learned how to engage in family, friendships, and community as well as stay engaged in heavenly matters. I spent ten years pastoring a church in my early twenties. During that time, I found the presence of God was tangible and available. I would often spend ten hours a day in prayer and worship.

Sometimes I would come home and go into my prayer room outside in the garage to spend half the night with Jesus. I was so in love and was so blessed that He would reveal His presence to me. In the midst of that, the Lord began to teach me how to engage with my family. I was not very good at loving on my kids in a meaningful way or understanding my wife's needs. I also wasn't very good at having healthy relationships in my church or with my leadership team.

God doesn't want heavenly minded prophets that are not healthy relationally. He does want prophets that are heavenly minded, but that can handle healthy relationships. In the next chapter, I want to delve into New Covenant prophets living in the tension of living from a heavenly place while fulfilling earth's mandates.

Chapter 17
Look For Prophets That Are In Community

One of the biggest challenges for a prophet is to live in a healthy community. The challenge with a prophet being extremely connected to spiritual encounters and heavenly matters is that they can begin to gain a bit of a superiority complex. They can start to think they are beyond the corporate leaders of their day. They can begin to feel like they have a theology that is superior, a way of living Christianity that is far advanced, and a relationship with God that is greater. That is immaturity at best and dangerous at worse.

I have had to fight through not being a "dangerous" and "immature" prophet myself. It is easier to live in heavenly places than to work on relationships, which often causes prophets to feel helpless. I've spent years in the church. I grew up passionate about God. I was leading people to Jesus at seven years old, filled with the Spirit and speaking in tongues. I even prayed and fasted at a young age. I conducted revivals and street witnessed before I was twenty and preached many times in the church and youth group. I was a worshiper from a young age and grew up playing music in the church. Needless to say, when I became a pastor with my newlywed Heather at 23, I was prepared for spiritual encounters, but I had much to learn in relationships and leadership.

One of my mentors said, "Keith, on a scale of 1 to 10, you are like a 10 concerning preaching and public ministry and a 3 or 4 in terms of relational health." The bottom line is that I wasn't very good at relationships. I was controlling, and afraid. I let people walk on me, and I walked on them. I hurt people and was hurt by people. I didn't know how to handle healthy confrontations, and I didn't know that healthy people had good boundaries. All of those skills didn't come easily. I resisted growing in relational health and instead would spend hours with Jesus on the piano and guitar in intercession. While I was growing with God, I wasn't growing in favor with man. The presence of the Lord was beginning to show up in our meetings and in my personal time with God, but relational immaturity was continually harming my growth and the development of our church.

I had grown up in churches where splits were commonplace. There didn't seem to be healthy ways of dealing with conflict. There was too big of a gap between the laity of the church and the leadership of the church. Leaders were taught to be friends only with those outside the congregation. They were taught that sheep bite; in other words, don't trust the people you lead. I believed all of it. It took me several years to begin to get healthy.

I used to say to myself that I was a prophet without honor in my hometown. When would God deliver me to a place where people received me? God had to keep me in that place to teach me how to overcome my lack of feeling honored and teach me how to create the culture of honor I wanted. I had to learn if I wanted to have honor, I needed to give honor. I couldn't demand that people value me if I wasn't first modeling I valued them. How can you value someone you don't trust? I was taught not to trust. So, I had to unlearn some lies and war with new truths. I had to believe that there was good in the body of Christ and that I could be a friend with people in my congregation. I found friends and fellowship, and by the end of our ten years in the pastoral ministry, I had begun to enjoy teamwork, leadership, friendship, healthy family and a healthy marriage.

We are looking for prophets that are healthy and in a community. That is the challenge and the discrepancy in the prophets of today. I see many prophets that have amazing ministries but aren't known in a home church community. I understand the challenges of being in a local community whether you are leading it or not. The last eight years, I have been a part of a local community in Vacaville, California and a part of the leadership team. I learned once I got here that it was much harder to find organic and healthy relationships not based on the function of ministry than I thought it would be. I was used to being the senior pastor and didn't realize that a lot of my relationships were built into my job. When I left the pastorate and joined the team in Vacaville, I realized I was at another level having to learn how to build community into my life.

I often find strength in my alone times with God. But I have come to realize over the last years how much I need interaction at a deep level with people outside of my immediate family. I definitely need healthy connections within my family, but I need friendships. I'm not very good at friendships that are not built around ministry, but it is an area I am fighting for and gaining victory.

I have heard over and over the despair of prophets who do not feel they have found their community or that they are not received. I believe most of the time they are believing a lie. I have seen over and over again the relational potential all around these individuals, but the lack of tools to get connected. They believe they must go somewhere else to find what they are looking for. Unfortunately, they will find that when they get to the next location, the same problem is resident, and the issue is still there.

This relational issue is the biggest problem and challenge we face today with prophetic people. Lack of ability to relate in healthy ways. I watched as reformers and revivalists disconnected from the church over the years and their message began to get more and more tainted. They may have a message of grace, but because of their inability to stay connected to a community of local believers in a healthy church, their frustrations with the church began to draw people away from the local body and into unhealthy elitism. They feel they carry a superior message and often even their message of grace has a sharp edge to it. How can a grace message not have the fruit of graciousness in its delivery? It can if the church has hurt you.

I am thankful for my wife, friends, and mentors that can spot when I am in an unhealthy place and call me on it, so I don't stay in that dysfunction. I was preaching on a book I put out a couple of years ago concerning the Father's heart. It was a whole series of meetings I was doing on learning to get into Kingdom family culture. My wife was there, and in the midst of me trying to communicate in the seminar, she spotted my problems. Even though people were telling me how blessed they were and encouraged to go deeper in meaningful father, son relationships, she identified that I had some bitterness I needed to deal with.

My words betrayed me during my messages. My wife can sometimes hear the spirit behind the word even if it seems I am saying the right thing. She notices when I am saying something with a stinger on it. It is kind of like Peter using his sword to cut off ears rather than to heal hearts. I was cutting off ears and sharing my frustrations with the church. Over the course of the next months, I was led to go through a season of deep inner healing to get another layer of hurts out of my heart that had accumulated over the course of the previous years. The Lord had been sharing with my wife that He wanted to promote me, but He was unable to do so if I didn't go through the necessary steps to get there. One of those steps included going through some inner healing. That inner healing led me to begin to believe some upgraded beliefs. I needed to pick up some godly beliefs and get some ungodly beliefs exposed in how I viewed God, people, peers, leaders, and the church.

I am so thankful that I went through that uncomfortable yet necessary season of healing. It was humbling, but it was so necessary. My wife and leaders around me noticed the drastic difference in my health since then, and some of those leaders looked to open doors of further Kingdom connections for me as a result of the increased level of health they saw in me. I have always appreciated and valued the room the Mission leaders have given me to grow in character while not pushing me out of the team. They have been an amazing example of God's grace to me and I'm forever grateful for them.

God is searching for healthy hearts to which he can entrust his prophetic ministries. Those we are seeking to be and to empower are those prophets who have chosen to get healthy. To be able to get into community, you first need to get healed. Healed hearts heal hearts. Unhealed hearts use the prophetic gift to hurt people and draw people out of healthy connections.

I have seen too many prophetic ministries taken out of commission because of warfare, demonic attacks, sickness, and relational lack of healthiness. Love covers. I believe that we would see much greater longevity of the prophets around us if we would be in a community. Peter was saved from the plans of Herod because he had a church that was praying for him. I believe if we are in community, we will have much more access to people that have our backs and are covering us in prayer.

In the next chapter, I want to talk about how healthy prophets are in a community and are a part of helping the church move into a greater expression of heaven on earth.

Chapter 18
Healthy Prophets Are A Part Of Helping The Church Move Forward

The church needs to move forward. I believe that we currently have a view of prophets that may inhibit this. We envision a prophet that is mad at the church, lives outside in a cave somewhere, and comes in and then leaves that church. He never has a relationship. We have a view that a prophet is not meant to be encumbered by relationships and needs to sustain a posture of aloofness to maintain honor.

As I have shared before, I have had the privilege of being a part of the leadership team at The Mission for the last eight years. Five of those years, I have been on the main core team at the church. Serving my local church in this way has been rewarding and I have grown leaps and bounds by being apart of this strong team. As a prophet, you can tend to have a perspective that you feel needs to be heard. In being on a local team you have to learn how to express your prophetic insights with wisdom and tact. Your words and life can have a more gradual impact. It seems that when you travel, more often than not your words impact differently and seemingly more quickly. Your words and ministry powerfully impact people, but at home, things often don't work the same way. Healthy change at home comes differently, sometimes slower.

I do believe God designed the majority of prophets to be in a healthy community at some level. He wants all prophets to be in communities of people that know them as a human being, a family member, and a member of the body of Christ. We all need to have a place where we are not seen as super-human all the time. I am so thankful that I have had a local team to run with that has seen and helped me in my areas of growth while still believing and calling out the best in me.

I have heard different reports of how valuable my input is into the church, including from our leadership team, but at times I have struggled to believe that is true. This is all apart of an emerging prophets journey into his place of influence. I remember one time I had a guest minister come into our church and preach a message I had been fighting for years to see infused into our church. It seemed that the process of my message was so sluggish in reaching our church culture. The minister from the outside was so well received that people clapped, cheered, and then fell in tears with much restoration as a result. I, on the other hand, was working through the grief that I hadn't been received in that very same message. This was probably my misperception, but it felt real then.

The guest minister honored me in front of the leadership gathering telling everyone that the reason that his message was so well received was because I had fought for that message in this church for years. He asked people to honor me and pray prayers of blessing over me. Although I was being honored at that moment, it didn't cause me to feel honored. Rather, that act of honor brought up the years of feeling misunderstood and not received. I cried as people honored me, not in appreciation, but hurt.

It can be hard for a prophet to understand how to walk the journey well in a local church. There may be challenges, misunderstandings, and feelings of not being received. This is all about our personal growth and getting healthier in how to present the messages we are passionate about as well as how to live under God's acceptance. We have to be willing to understand that God wants us in a local church. We must learn to realize that progress is happening in our midst, but it is slower at times than we would like. If we could learn to see that good things are indeed happening, we could go the distance.

I have had to learn how to be thankful for what is occurring in our midst. I have had to fight to appreciate where people are at and not judge them. I have also had to learn to recognize that I am not the only answer to what God is doing in our midst. I am a piece of the puzzle. That was a great breakthrough for me. I only see in part as a prophet. It takes a variety of perspectives to see the work of a local community thrive. As much as I am passionate about the piece that I see, I have had to and continually need to remind myself that I bring one perspective to the table.

One of the things that I have chosen to do, while experiencing frustration that my point of view is not being heard, is to work at understanding and valuing perspectives of others that I don't consider as valuable. On several occasions, I have chosen to work with team members that I don't particularly appreciate their type of work at the same level they do. I have believed that the way I work is of greater value, even though that is not true. It is the challenge at times for prophets. It is in these moments that I have chosen to spend time working alongside others I don't fully see from their perspective until I catch a glimpse of why they do what they do. I have experienced that as I have come towards understanding others' perspectives, then I see them beginning to approach my point of view as well. It is worth it, but it is not easy to get there.

Healthy prophets are in healthy connections and fight for healthy relationships. In doing this, prophets are then entrusted with the task of moving the church forward. I have seen numerous local prophets attempting to advance the church through things that they see. The things they see are good, but the inability to understand how they are being received and how much they can alter the course of the church sometimes eludes them. It is mutually challenging for leaders to have the grace to listen to the prophets that are amongst them. Leaders at times feel challenged, devalued, and disrespected if a prophetic word is presented in the wrong way, or if the message is delivered in a condescending manner, often unbeknownst by the prophet.

I have been invited to speak by some leaders into their churches, by other leaders into their businesses, and by others into their unique venues. One thing I have learned is that just because you are invited to speak into things doesn't mean that what you are going to speak will be fully received. Neither should what you say be fully listened to, accepted and embraced. Prophets need to be tested because the best prophets only see in part. The most immature prophets only see problems. It takes a mature prophet to recognize what to say, when to say it, how to say it, and who to say it to. If we are to be a part of those that speak into others that invite us in, we must learn to listen to the spirit of wisdom.

I have seen too many casualties in the church and in the world where prophetic voices have tried to speak into things and haven't been fully received. Either the leaders they speak into pull away or push them away. The prophets can also pull away if they feel they are not heard fully, or even leave the church they are a part of if they don't feel like their voice is completely valued. I have had to learn that my voice is valuable, but it is not the only voice. I am glad that at times the things I spoke into didn't turn out exactly as I thought they would. I am glad areas that I warned about didn't happen as I warned they would. I am pleased when people that I didn't feel were trustworthy ended up becoming trustworthy vessels. Now sometimes it was my words of warning, wisdom, or caution that caused another leader to see the potential pitfalls and to structure things accordingly, thus avoiding potential pitfalls. But I realize at times that I was only partially seeing the picture. It takes a courageous leader to be able to weight the words of the prophets without throwing out that prophet and also still maintaining relationship with them.

Each prophet must be secure in who they are in God if they are to stay in the relational game to be a part of shaping the church. I have seen prophets that are no longer in the church dynamic at all because they have gotten hurt by the shortcomings of a given church. I know there are many deficiencies in churches. The goal is to learn to stay together despite disagreements. There may be a time when a prophet should leave a church, but it shouldn't be in reaction to hurt, bitterness, or anger. It should be because the Lord has promoted them to another location or it is better to move to a different culture where there is a better and more similar DNA.

I have encouraged prophets who want to give up on a church or a system in the world that is faulty to stay in the game. I ask them how can that system change if you are only speaking about what is wrong with it from the outside?

You need to be on the inside to be a part of helping build a bridge from where that organization is to where it needs to be. That takes time. It is worth it because we are dreaming of better ways of doing things that need a prophet's help to get it there.

I am dreaming of a day where prophets are healthy, apostles and prophets work well together, prophets aren't loners, prophets are in a community, and prophets primarily encourage, comfort, build, exhort, revive, and reform. I am looking for a day when leaders of local churches see and fully value the prophets that are emerging amongst them and at times within themselves. I am looking for the day when we can recognize there doesn't need to be just one icon prophet per church or organization, but God designed companies of prophets to function together for the sake of a region. I am dreaming of a day when prophets are whole, free of bitterness, building the church and not tearing it down. I am dreaming of a day when prophets partner with the church to see the lost saved, cities restored, sin-filled places filled with light, and heaven come to earth. I am dreaming about emerging prophets. I am dreaming about you.

Stay in the game; believe in those that are emerging around you. If you are an emerging prophet, don't give up. We can change the landscape of how people see prophets. You can become one of the healthy prophets that give the church and the world hope again. God is dreaming about you becoming healthy and so am I.

God bless you.

For More Information

Please take a look at our website www.emergingprophets.com to find out how you can sign up for a module on our online school or attend a regional emerging prophet school near you. If you are interested in personally being developed as an emerging prophet we also offer coaching for developing prophets, as well as marketplace leaders. If you are interested in hosting an Emerging Prophet weekend intensive to introduce the concept of developing prophets in your area please contact us. Also if you are interested in starting an emerging prophet school in your area we would love to chat with you to see if this would be a good fit for you and us. Also if you would like to have Keith Ferrante or one of the emerging prophet trainers out to minister in your church or venue please contact us through the emerging prophets website.

Made in the USA
Monee, IL
19 November 2020